Military
Miniatures

Military Miniatures

Simon Goodenough
and 'Tradition'

Chilton Book Company
Radnor, Pennsylvania

Published in 1978 in the USA by
Chilton Book Company, Radnor, Pennsylvania
and simultaneously in Don Mills, Ontario, Canada by
Thomas Nelson & Sons, Ltd. All rights reserved.
© Orbis Publishing Limited, London and
Istituto Geografico de Agostini, Novara 1977
Printed in Italy by IGDA, Novara

*Cover: Units of the Light Brigade charge down the
Valley of Death at Balaclava in 1854. Photograph:
Mike Foster. Endpapers: The uniform of the
Coldstream Guards in 1856. From left to right:
Major, Night sentry, Drummer, Barrack guard, Drum
major, Colour sergeant, Drill sergeant and Night sentry*

*Title page: A selection of 80-mm and 90-mm
figures from the* Tradition *range dating from 1700
to 1944. Back row, left to right: General von
Seydlitz of Prussia (1750); an officer of the 2nd
Dutch Lancers of the French Imperial Guard (1815);
Benito Mussolini. Centre: an officer of the French
Line Infantry in Spain (c. 1808); General de La
Motte-Fouque (1750); Grenadier of the Guards
Battalion No 15 of Prussia (1750). Front row:
Frederick the Great; the Duke of Marlborough; an
officer of the 42nd Highlanders, the Black Watch
(1815); Marshal Bessières, French (c. 1810–12)*

ISBN 0-8019-6721-X *Hardcover*
ISBN 0-8019-6722-8 *Paperbound*
Library of Congress Catalog Card Number 77-93021

The publishers would like to acknowledge the help of
the following in permitting the use of photographs
shown on the pages listed.

Carlo Bevilacqua: 14, 15, 16, 17, 18, 20, 21, 22,
    32, 34.
A. C. Cooper: 36.
Derek Cross: 12, 30, 54, 66.
Historex: 25 bottom
India Office Library/Photo Fleming: 39.
Mansell Collection: 44 bottom right.
F. A. Mella: 18.
National Army Museum: 38, 83.
National Army Museum/Chris Barker: 81.
Lt-Col. J. B. R. Nicholson: 37 top left, 40, 42, 43, 44,
    top right, 45.
Philip Stearns: 23, 24, 25 top, 26, 28, 29, 33.
Tallandier: 40, 41.
Victoria and Albert Museum: 37 top right.

The author is grateful for the help afforded by the work of
Massimo Alberini in the preparation of this book.

Studio photography by Peter Pugh-Cook.
Drawings by Pam Hardman
Designed by Ingrid Mason

Contents

Foreword

This book is not just about collecting model soldiers, it is a book about craftsmanship; it describes how to paint miniatures, how to mould and cast them and how to alter them to suit your own requirements. As some knowledge of history is important to the accuracy of military miniatures, the book takes a brief look at the main changes in fashion over the last few hundred years and gives some idea of the range of military uniforms as well as how to go about researching them in accurate detail. This is primarily a practical book, however; it sets out to teach you how to become a model-maker yourself.

There are many companies, large and small, that make model soldiers. Through this book a professional model-maker from *Tradition,* one of the best-known of these firms, gives general advice on model-making and works through several different projects step by step, explaining in detail the kind of equipment you will need and how to use it. He explains a great many points that should enable you, with some practice, to produce work of a very high standard.

Tradition is the trade name for a firm called Norman Newton Limited that makes and markets beautifully crafted model soldiers. The firm has a shop in Mayfair, London, in which it sells its own soldiers; it also supplies other shops and wholesalers in many countries, and the craftsmen who work there make one-off figures for collectors. It also sells military antiques and, until recently, it had its own military magazine, also called *Tradition*.

Since 1950, when the firm began, it has developed from two men making and selling three or four model soldiers a week to a world-wide concern. The two men were Roy Belmont-Maitland and Charles Stadden. Stadden made the figures and Belmont-Maitland sold them. The task confronting the new firm was to launch on to what was basically a market primarily concerned with toys, an image of the model soldier as a commercially available collector's item. *Tradition* still sells the famous Stadden figures but their master craftsman is now Alan Caton whose hands you can see at work painting a figure in the photograph on the opposite page. He has worked through the projects shown later in this book. His experience, we hope, will encourage you to produce your own work and develop a new practical skill which will give great pleasure and satisfaction.

SIMON GOODENOUGH

7

Introduction

Model soldiers are much more than toys and attract an ever-growing interest among people of all ages. Their popularity is richly fed by a wide variety of contributing interests, which appeal to many different types of people: the collector, the artist, the hobby-enthusiast, the historian, the games-player, the craftsman, the antiquarian and the romantic. Each one of these people finds something in model soldiers to satisfy him personally.

The collector admires the accurate detail and superb workmanship of the miniature figures. The craftsman and hobby-enthusiast devote hours of concentration to kits and figures which they painstakingly put together or transform with knife, file and solder. The artist draws endless satisfaction from painting a figure in the exact colours and details of the dress of 100 or 1,000 years ago. The wargame enthusiast is preoccupied with the problems of reversing the decisions of Blenheim, Waterloo, Pharsalus or Gettysburg with massed ranks in table-top battles. Anyone with a feeling for history, colour or pageantry will be immersed in research among the vast collections of museums and libraries, delving into old prints, paintings, photographs, memoirs and personal records.

This book shows all these aspects of model soldiers. The first part gives a brief history of the model soldier since Egyptian times and discusses the different types of models, in paper, flat metal, half-rounded, hollow, solid and in plastic. It also gives some idea of the variety of periods available on the market and some of the names of the craftsmen whose work can be found. There are hints on how to set about making and displaying a collection and suggestions on how to start researching into the historical details of uniform and background. An effort has been made to give some feeling of the scope and variety of material available in the wealth of different uniforms throughout history. We have also made some suggestions of the periods of history which might be of particular interest both to collectors and to wargame enthusiasts. The span of the subject is so great that any one book can only give a taste of it.

Left: A trumpeter of the Saxon Guard Reiter regiment. This is a 90-mm figure

A later part of the book works through several practical projects with the help of Alan Caton. He shows how to put a simple kit together and how to paint a figure, a horse and a piece of artillery. He then demonstrates how to adapt or convert figures by changing the angle of the arms, legs, head or torso, as well as how to recreate a completely new figure from a different period in history and of another nationality. Alan Caton starts with a simple conversion and goes on to a remarkable conversion in which five identical troopers of the British dragoon guards of 1900 are reshaped into a group of five completely different figures at Custer's Last Stand at the Battle of Little Big Horn.

Alan Caton gives advice on the materials and instruments needed to make these conversions and suggests his own methods step-by-step. He also explains how to display groups of figures in dioramas with naturalistic backgrounds and how to make landscapes, trees, the appearance of water, lighting effects and buildings. There is a project on moulding and casting a figure so that a collection could start from the very beginning— from a ball of plasticene in the hand.

All the projects use metal soldiers made out of combinations of lead and tin and make use of solder for conversions. Plastic soldiers are very popular today particularly as miniature wargame figures, as toys or as kits consisting of 50 or 60 component parts aimed at the hobby-enthusiast. Painting a plastic figure demands as much skill as painting a metal figure and is done in the same way so you will be able to follow the instructions in this book if you have a plastic figure you want to paint.

The metal figure, however, is more versatile since it covers a much wider range of periods. A collector of model soldiers will usually collect metal soldiers, not plastic ones. In addition to buying metal kits, you can exercise your hobby instinct by converting metal figures and cheap miniature metal figures can be bought for wargames, although wargame figures can also be very satisfactory collectors' items. The metal figure appeals to every taste and every pocket. Many people come into the hobby through plastic figures and then go on to metal figures, which have been hand animated.

We hope this book will confirm your interest in model soldiers. Wargames, dioramas, original uniforms and beautifully created models are all ways to capture new interest. Not only the bow-fronted shop-window of *Tradition* but the windows of many other model soldier shops are packed with material to excite the curiosity of passers-by. They pause for many reasons. Some see Alan Caton at work and stop to admire the skill that goes into his figures. Someone may remember that he had an uncle in a certain regiment and enquires on the spur of the moment whether there is a model of that regiment in the shop. If there is not, one can be made. Another has memories of playing with hollow *Britains* (a make of model soldier) when he was young and is amazed to see how much more variety there is today.

Young enthusiasts reel off lists of specialist requirements, naming obscure regiments with an amazing facility. Americans, Germans, Frenchmen and Japanese make special stopovers and exchange anecdotes about their own collections or merely about themselves. There are those who come regularly to check up on the latest models and those who come tentatively to choose a difficult present. Some know just what they want, others are only looking.

Most people respond to the miniature detail in the figures, which is shown to its best advantage in the painted model, complete with the trappings of its uniform. It was the uniforms that first caught

Above: Colonel Kelly of the 2nd Guards stands on the left of the picture and, on the right, is Lord Combermere, of the 2nd Lifeguards

Right: Sapeur of the French line infantry, about the year 1812

Roy Belmont-Maitland's attention. The colour of real uniforms contrasted brilliantly with the grey poverty of the inter-war depression, seemingly the only flash of colour in life. He was hooked from the moment he first discovered old prints and pictures. As a child, he would press his face against shop-windows behind which prints were sold that he could not afford and would gaze in admiration at uniforms hired out as costumes for parties or even sold as second-hand working clothes.

Toy soldiers were the nearest he could come to the real uniforms he coveted, so he developed a passion for boxes of flats and *Britains*, which were all that any child could afford. Much later he was able to develop his obsession for collecting military antiques. His interest in model soldiers is still dictated by his over-riding interest in real uniforms and he manages to combine those two interests with great success. He feels sure that the interest of many people must be caught in a similar way, not always at first perhaps by the models themselves but often by some other aspect of military history.

The charge of the Royal Scots Greys and the 92nd Gordon Highlanders at the Battle of Waterloo, 18th June 1815. This is another part of the diorama created by Derek Cross also shown on pages 66 and 67

Four Thousand Years

In the history of military miniatures, model soldiers have been found in Egyptian tombs and have been employed to train kings and generals in the art of war

There is no record in modern times of a monarch or general requiring to be buried with a bodyguard of model soldiers. Some collectors might grieve at this surprising gap in the potential market. Four thousands years ago, however, the Egyptians found such models a sound economy.

Princes were not supposed to lie empty-handed or unprotected in their tombs and so food and precious jewels were laid beside them to ensure their material comforts and servants and guards were buried with them to guarantee a safe journey through the afterlife. But living—or, rather, dead—guards could be a costly waste. Symbolic models were far cheaper and may even have been thought more powerful, so in time they superseded dead guards.

The first known military models were found in the tomb of Prince Emsah, a successful Egyptian warrior who lived about 2000 BC and was buried at Assiut in Upper Egypt. Emsah took no risks in death, whatever fortunes he pursued in life. He was guarded by two groups of painted wooden figures: one group Egyptian, the other Numidian. The Numidians often fought as Egypt's allies, their bowmen were lightly armed and quick on their feet, the perfect adjunct to the heavier Egyptian infantry armed with javelins and shields. The bright patterns of the Numidian loin-cloths still show clearly on the figures.

Ritual burial of model soldiers does not seem to have outlasted such ancient times, perhaps because people lost faith in their effectiveness. There are few examples of any kind of military figures in the first millenium AD. A few toys, a Roman legionary made of tin, two tin knights—not much survived the dark ages of the medieval European turmoil and we have little idea of the purpose even these examples served.

It was in the emergence from that medieval chaos that miniature figures came into their own once more. In classical and medieval times war for most people was a matter of survival. The threat of death was a way of life. Later, as Europe became 'enlightened', in the seventeenth and eighteenth centuries, war became a business, with complex rules and carefully formulated plans and stratagems. Princes had no wish to die or to be

Above: A strong detachment of Egyptian heavy infantry with lances and shields from the tomb of Prince Emsah, a soldier of fortune in the 12th Egyptian Dynasty. These painted wooden figures are about 4,000 years old

buried with their troops either in the flesh or in the shape of models. Instead they learnt the art of war with fond concentration, deploying table-top troops in theoretical manoeuvres and exchanging endless arguments on the practical philosophy of sacrificing the lives of others.

The sacrifices they made with models after dinner, they made on the field with the flick of a scented handkerchief. Blood was spilled as if it had been an excess of snuff shaken from the back of the hand. The French and the British confronted each other on the battlefield and each politely invited the other to take the first shot. The monarchs of Europe argued out their birthrights. Nations struggled for identity. A new philosophy tried to grace everyday dealings in death with high-sounding theories of order and method. The bright dash of uniforms attempted to conceal the dull waste of war.

A few kings and commanders commissioned priceless collections of model soldiers. One of the most valuable was owned by Louis XIII of France, for whom it was made on the instructions of his mother. Having inherited and added to this collection, Louis XIV was forced to sell it for the sake of its silver content, in order to fund those wars for which he had practised with the models—a vicious circle of need and greed. Other monarchs who owned marvellous collections over the next two centuries included Napoleon III's heir, the Prince Imperial, and King Ferdinand II of Naples. The practice of using model soldiers as the means to rehearse real-life situations was continued in the Prussian military academies of the nineteenth century and even by the Japanese in the Second World War.

At the time of Louis XIV it was only the very wealthy who could afford to indulge themselves with model soldiers. It was not until a century later that the first commercial manufacturers began to tap an ever-widening market. By mixing tin with lead or copper they were able to produce models that the public could afford.

Interest among the public grew partly because of the availability of a cheaper product and partly because of a growing obsession with the elaborate paraphernalia of war. The diversity and brilliance of uniforms attracted and dazzled everyone with their display of decorative fashion. In the late eighteenth century boys of 15 and 16 were recruited through pamphlets which blatantly extolled the detailed splendours of the uniforms to which they would become entitled if they signed up in the king's service.

Enormous sums of money were lavished on the glamorous appearance and proud bearing of European armies, each composed of many individual troops with their individual characteristics of manners and uniforms. States, armies and soldiers found themselves constantly re-adjusting their alliances in the complex quarrels of the seventeenth, eighteenth and nineteenth centuries. In the course of their travels they found themselves ex-

changing ideas and borrowing fashions of uniform in such a web of interbreeding that the most idiosyncratic characteristics of dress became a common sight in almost every European city. It was hardly surprising that the mania for uniform found a reflection in the revival of the model soldier and that the periods of greatest interest to collectors were the periods of the richest variety of military uniform—the armies of Frederick the Great and Napoleon Bonaparte.

It was Frederick's father, known as the Sergeant King, who laid the basis for the efficiency and success of Frederick's own armies. When the Sergeant King lay dying, his last wish was to watch his bodyguard march past the end of his bed in

Above: Numidian light infantry armed with short lances, also from the tomb of Prince Emsah—these were not in fact toys but funeral grave-goods, essential guardians of the dead warrior in the afterlife. The figures are now in the Cairo Museum having been found during excavations at Assiut in Upper Egypt

ARTILLERIE avec Canons

Trompette   Trompette   Capitaine   Maréchal des Logis   Artilleur   Artilleur

CANON ATTELÉ

Lieutenant   Brigadier   Artilleur   Sous-Lieut. Porte Étendard   Artilleur   Artilleur

Servants   CANON en BATTERIE   Attelages

full military splendour. The impressive sight of their uniforms and their noble stature reassured him in his last moments.

There may be those today who foster just such a dream but they will have to make do with soldiers of a less vital substance, made of paper, plastic or metal. The history of model soldiers between the start of their commercial production and the First World War is the story of their development from flat figures in paper and metal to three-dimensional shapes in metal. The changing popularity of flats, paper figures, half-round or *mezzo-tondo* figures, fully round or *ronde-bosse* figures and three-dimensional hollow metal figures depended partly on national habit but even more on considerations of cost and the model's function, either as a toy or as a show piece.

Left: A printed sheet of cavalry and artillery of the French Second Empire by the Imagerie Pellerin of Epinal. These sheets could be cut up and the soldiers pasted onto board so that they could stand, or the sheets could be presented as they were. The popularity of these sheets dates back to the Napoleonic Empire

Below: Two more sheets from the Imagerie Pellerin. At the top, a splendid set of Italian cavalrymen and, at the bottom, an officer and men of the Italian Bersaglieri

From paper sheets to hollow *Britains*

Strasbourg in France and Nuremberg in Germany are the two towns associated with the birth of paper and flat soldiers. Inspired by the interest shown by the citizens of Strasbourg in the troops of the visiting Louis XV in 1744, the printer Seyfried quickly produced some souvenir sheets of the soldiers and hawked them round the streets. They sold remarkably well. Other printers took up the idea and the popularity of paper soldiers spread to other towns. The Pellerin brothers, who worked at Epinal in the Vosges, became the best known manufacturers and produced some of their best material during the Napoleonic wars.

The printed sheets developed into smaller cut-out soldiers that could be stuck on cardboard or wood and used as toys. At first wood blocks were used for printing and the painting of the soldiers was done by hand. Some of the figures might occasionally be coloured with gold trappings for wealthy patrons but on the whole the basic sheets were fairly cheap. They were certainly the cheapest kind of model soldiers available to a child and they remained popular until this century.

In the collection of King Ferdinand of Naples there was one procession of 2,000 paper figures, representing lords and ladies of the Bourbon court, the uniforms of the Kingdom of Naples and detachments of the Italian army of the time. These are now in the San Martino Museum in Naples.

Four thousand years

Above: Piedmontese infantry from the San Martino Museum in Naples. These are individually hand-painted paper models by Filippo Gin, a Neapolitan artist born in 1845

Right: A collection of old Britain *figures. The ones here include Guardsmen and Gordon Highlanders*

Below: These Teutonic knights are modern castings from original moulds of the famous Nuremberg flats. They are only a few millimetres thick but they still show an amazing amount of detail

There are also collections of paper soldiers in the Musée de l'Armée in Paris and in the Army Museum in Madrid.

Flat metal soldiers appeared at the beginning of the seventeenth century but they were first sold in quantity by a metal founder called Hilpert who moved to Nuremberg and set up a family business producing thin, flat metal soldiers that were sold either painted or unpainted. The best known of his imitators and successors was Ernst Heinrichsen, who established his own family business, also in Nuremberg. Heinrichsen organized the Nuremberg flats, as they became known, into an industry, and these model soldiers dominated the market from about 1830 to 1890. The soldiers were made in regular sizes of 30 or 40 millimetres and sold in boxes by weight. One kg (2·2 pounds) in weight represented about 330 soldiers. The boxes were colourful, the figures were carefully packed already fixed to their bases and accessories such as trees and cannon could also be bought.

These flats were really toys but they were often beautifully painted by collectors. There was barely any relief on them in the early years of production but when the relief was later increased the figures contained nearly as much detail as a fully rounded

figure. With careful shading and colouring—and viewed from the right angle—they could look as good as any three-dimensional shape.

Semi-solids were the next step. They became popular in the second half of the nineteenth century. As their name implies they were thicker than the flats and could obviously have more detail worked on them. They were a sort of half-way stage between flats and fully rounded figures and, like the flats, have always been more popular in Germany than anywhere else. Allgeyer and Schweizer were two of the earliest craftsmen of the semi-rounds and later Kober of Vienna made a wide and well-deserved reputation for himself with semi-rounds.

The French have never been very keen on flats or semi-rounds. In the year of the French Revolution a metal worker called Lucotte produced fully rounded soldiers which were known as Lucotte's 'little men'. Later the trademark *C.B.G.* produced exciting boxes of fully rounded figures. *C.B.G.* stood for the craftsmen Cuberly, Blondel and Gerbeau. You can still buy *C.B.G.* models today because Mignot, another Frenchman, took over the firm and developed it as *C.B.G. Mignot.* He was one of the few Frenchmen who also produced flat figures.

The British did not enter the game until 1893 when an English maker of mechanical toys, who was appropriately called Britain, decided to compete with the German flats and the French solids

Above: Half round or mezzo-tondo *figures from moulds made by the Schweizer family. The figures represent a French soldier being taken before a Prussian general after Prussia's victory in 1871*

Right: Box-showcases of flats by C.B.G. Mignot, *with the same background serving several purposes. At the top, the meeting between Joan of Arc and the Dauphin; below that, knights facing halberdiers and crossbowmen. At the bottom, two scenes from Napoleon's invasion of Egypt*

by producing cheaper hollow figures. His soldiers were known as *Britains* and they became very popular indeed. There are probably many *Britains* still lying in dusty attics.

The standard *Britain* was 54 mm high and was hollow cast from thin lead alloy. The figures, being hollow, used much less lead, which was why they were cheaper. They were mainly British but covered a wide range of regiments and were made with great accuracy of detail and painted with efficient care. Revised versions of earlier productions were often put on the market. For example, the tail of the first version of a camel in the camel corps was made of wire, but the second version had a lead tail. The tremendous output stopped in 1967, since when *Britains* have been making plastic figures.

Four thousand years

Metal models today

In the first half of this century men's minds were occupied with conflicts more universal than any table-top general of preceding centuries could have anticipated. War was no longer a series of incidents colourfully or tragically performed at a safe distance from the homeland, as the colonial wars of the last half of the nineteenth century had been. Suddenly war was a world-wide catastrophe that forced its way into everyone's lives. There was no time for sentimentalizing over the past.

There was a serious shortage of metal after World War I and by the time it was available again children were more interested in the mechanical delights of the twentieth century than in model soldiers. The new collecting mania was for motor cars and railway engines. Germany itself was forbidden to make military toys of any kind, under a clause in the Treaty of Versailles. It is partly because of that clause that German flats still lay more emphasis on civilian figures than do the model miniatures of any other country.

When, towards the beginning of World War II, interest in model soldiers once more grew beyond flats and Britains, methods of working developed differently in different countries. In France, for example, master figure-makers tend to be commissioned by individual clients, which can also happen in Britain and America but with far less regularity. In both these countries there are small

Above: Two of the original Mignot *figures representing different uniforms of the French Revolutionary Army of 1792*

Below left: This is a collector's piece, a military miniature as opposed to a toy, made by Fernande Métayer of Paris. Superbly accurate and detailed, the figure represents an officer of Napoleon's Grenadiers à cheval. Each part, horse and rider, would have been cast separately

firms in which one man is producing his own figures on request. There are also larger firms, like *Tradition* in Britain and *Imrie-Risley* in America, which have long lists of commercially available figures which have been created for them by several independent master figure-makers commissioned by the firm. The only such firm in France is *C.B.G. Mignot.* These larger firms often use their own master figure-maker to make a manikin figure which is then animated and painted by outside workers on behalf of the firm.

The master figure-makers are the creative element behind the vast output of model soldiers, whether plastic or metal. The best of them produce wholly original figures. Some produce clearly recognizable adaptations of the work of others. Inevitably some work is good, some not so good. If you have an eye for detail, you will soon begin to tell the difference. A list of the better-known craftsmen would be very long and you can get an idea of the variety of work available from the names of just a few of the best.

Collectors' pieces were produced in limited numbers between the wars by Richard Courtenay, who concentrated on making superb figures of medieval knights in armour from the time of the Black Prince to Henry V, spanning the Hundred Years War between England and France. His heraldry is extremely accurate; the colours of his figures are bright and they usually seem to be involved in plenty of action.

Right: These cleverly conceived figures are by Charles Stadden. They represent Napoleon offering a pinch of snuff to a Grenadier of the Old Guard. The figures are in the collection of Peter Blum

Below: French dragoon of the seventeenth century made by Eugène Leliepvre. This figure is 40 cm (16 inches) tall and has a uniform made of real cloth, stitched by hand —to work in this sort of detail the dimensions must be greater

In France, the serious collector had several excellent sources from the 1940s onward. When Madame Fernande Métayer suddenly found that she had to make her own living she began to research military figures and quickly adapted her interest in water-colours to painting figures which she commissioned from sculptors who worked to her original designs. Her reputation has grown partly through her own figures and partly through those she has created together with Lucien Rousselot, a designer, figurine maker and water colour artist who was commissioned at one time to do a series of plates now much sought after as sources of reference, of the uniforms and arms of the French army.

Immaculate research and amazing detail are also the style of Mademoiselle Josianne des Fontaines, who is spoken of as one of the finest of all the modern craftsmen. She spent two years making a Carthaginian War scene complete with elephants. She also makes civilian scenes, one of which is a sequence taken from the life of Casanova.

Eugène Leliepvre often works in collaboration with Mademoiselle des Fontaines. Like Rousselot he has also been an official French artist. His concern for detail is so precise that he made a 40-cm figure of a French dragoon of the seventeenth century with a uniform made of cloth and stitched along the seams exactly where the original coat would have been stitched.

Unlike the commercial figures, these individually produced masterpieces are always unique. Roger Berdou and Frederick Ping also concentrate on figures made to individual order. Frederick Ping took over the Courtenay figures and still produces many medieval models. Instead of casting in one piece he often builds a figure up with solder and pieces of sheet lead on to a prototype model so that every model is different.

The best of the commercial figures are also collectors' items. Apart from the skilled craftsmanship and detail of the figures made by Charles Stadden, they are also remarkable for the range of history they cover. Some of his most famous early figures were of the Indian Cavalry of the nine-

23

teenth century but he has also created figures ranging from Roman times through the Middle Ages, Frederick the Great, the American War of Independence, the British of Napoleonic times and the armies of the late nineteenth century up to the British and German armies of World War II.

Certain names are associated with certain characteristic figures. Russell Gammage and his *Rose* models made his reputation with models commemorating the Coronation of the Queen of England in 1953. Now he produces a range from classical times to World War II. John Greenwood was famous for his British line regiments. Marcus Hinton made a wide variety of medieval armoured figures, as well as figures from the Crimean War, the American Revolution and the Napoleonic era. Frank Hinchcliffe has a wide reputation for the

Left: Excellent detail and an expressive face in a figure of Marshal Bessières, one of Napoleon's marshals, by Charles Stadden. This is a 54-mm figure in the collection of J. Linen

Below: Russell Gammage made these figures of the Egyptian Pharaoh Thutmose III riding into battle in his war chariot, which show great historical accuracy of detail. The figures, mounted and painted by Donald Burgess, are in the collection of Philip Stearns

excellence of his artillery pieces, horse teams and weapons, as well as other figures.

Groups of figures in battle situations or informal poses are known as dioramas. Some craftsmen specialize in creating these set pieces. For example, there is Edward Surén, who began his 'Willie' figures in about 1964 and makes a range of individual figures from Romans and Normans to Napoleonic and Franco-Prussian. He has also made a reputation for himself with his massed figures in dioramas of such events as Rorke's Drift, from the Zulu War of 1879, Marshal Ney's heavy cavalry charging the British at Quatre Bras at the opening to the campaign that culminated in the Battle of Waterloo, and Ticonderoga, at which the French and British colonial troops confronted each other in Canada in 1759.

In America, *Imrie-Risley* concentrate on the American War of Independence and the American Civil War. *Valiant* miniatures produce excellent kits while *Vallance* provide one-piece castings with weapons that have to be separately fixed to the model.

Individual modellers are the main focus of attention in America. Modellers such as Shep Paine attain a very high standard of work in their exhibitions but they are not commercial.

The main historical emphasis in America is on the Civil War in preference to the War of Independence, with which the majority of Americans have more difficulty in relating. The battle sites of the

Above: The battle between French and British colonial troops at Ticonderoga, 1759. Edward Surén created this diorama. It is perfect in detail right down to the construction of the gabions which are the wicker baskets packed with earth from the trenches

Below: A French lancer makes off with the spoils of war—an imaginative reconstruction with a Historex *figure*

War of Independence lie mostly along the line of the East Coast megalopolis, buried now beneath concrete and skyscrapers. The Civil War is not only more recent but it ranged over a far wider area. Almost every battle site has some small memorial or museum as a constant reminder of things past but not to be forgotten.

Plastic figures

The use of plastic introduced an entirely new and exciting aspect into the world of model soldiers. Plastic figures were first produced in quantity by a Pole called Zang, who started *Heralds* and later amalgamated with *Britains*. As metal figures catered increasingly for the collector, plastic figures took over the role of toys that had once been played by flat and hollow figures. The *Swoppet* range that was produced by *Britains-Herald* contained a variety of medieval knights with interchangeable heads, belts, and weapons. The knights even had torsos that could be split up and swopped around.

Plastic figures quickly became much more than toys. They began to appeal to the serious hobby instinct of many model soldier enthusiasts. For example, the French firm of *Historex* now supply plastic kits with up to 60 component parts to be assembled at home. Although instructions are provided, just how you fix the angles of the limbs—

Above: Figures by Imrie-Risley *representing Union cavalry dismounted and in action at the Battle of Gettysburg, 1863*

Right: British officer of the 12th Royal Lancers about the year 1900

as well as many other details—can be up to your own inclination. This is real do-it-yourself work. A professionally finished and painted *Historex* figure can be a collector's item but it can also require just as much labour as modifying and painting a solid metal figure.

The British firm of *Airfix* go in for the very smallest figures, down to 18 or 20 mm. Their 48-man packs are ideal for people who collect figures for wargames. The larger size *Elastolin* models of Romans and later periods are a modern plastic revival from a firm that once made its figures from papier mâché and later progressed to sawdust, resin and glue.

These are just some of the types of figures you can buy, and this is just a starting point. The figures themselves represent only the surface of a world that will rapidly absorb you in its depths and range of interest. Having made your first few choices, you will want to know much more about that world, and will soon find yourself collecting in earnest, diligently researching the details of the figures you have bought, planning how to display them in battleground reconstructions.

Collecting Model Soldiers

An odd assortment of figures can lead to a beautiful collection of which you may justly be proud. There are many ways of displaying miniature soldiers to their best advantage and many great collections from which you can seek inspiration

The hobby enthusiast draws his greatest pleasure from putting a kit together or adapting a figure to his own requirements. The collector on the other hand generally gains more pleasure from the display that he can make with his figures, whether singly or in groups.

Even the serious collectors can no longer afford to buy examples of every kind of work produced, as they once used to, due to the present range of figures available. The average collector is certainly going to have to think out the limits of his collection very carefully to suit his pocket. Space is also a problem; one shelf does not hold many soldiers. So collections must be planned fairly strictly.

Most collectors begin with an assortment of pieces that they might have gathered over several years. This may include a few Napoleonic figures, some classical pieces, a medieval knight or two bought in a burst of enthusiasm and possibly some twentieth century pieces. When they find that space forces them to relegate their earliest pieces to a cupboard in order to make room for their latest aquisitions, then they may begin to wonder how they can make a more permanent show of their models. Placed together without plan the assortment may look a real mess. Different periods and different scales will make the whole group look a little absurd. That is the time to start planning what to buy next.

If you are really interested in the quality of the workmanship you may well decide to select examples of the very best available figures. In that case you will probably find yourself referring to some of the names which have already been mentioned, although of course there are many other excellent craftsmen. Or you may find that there is one particular craftsman whose work you admire and you will concentrate your collection on him.

You may have an eye for the rare and antique, or a sentimental attachment to *Britains*. Old *Britains* can still be bought, so can old flats, half flats and fully-rounded figures but you will find yourself paying antique-rated prices for them. Alternatively you can buy modern flats, which will certainly solve some of your problems if you have only a limited amount of space.

If you are going to collect modern pieces rather than period pieces then you have a stunning variety of choice and several decisions to make unless you wish to find yourself swamped by soldiers. There are several questions you must ask yourself, firstly are you going to collect one example of every period from Ur to Ulster or will you concentrate on a single period? If you choose one period, are you going to collect all the nationalities of that period or merely examples of all the regiments of one nationality?

You must also decide whether you want variety or a massed British square; whether you want to gather together all the protagonists at one battle, such as Waterloo, or stretch yourself over the medieval knights of the Hundred Year's War, the Europeans of the Thirty Years War, or the Prussians and Austrians of the Seven Years War. You must choose between cavalry and infantry. Alternatively you may want a collection of the principle generals of history: Napoleon, Marlborough, von Seydlitz,

Opposite page: A magnificent figure by Ray Lamb animated from a Historex *kit. The final figure is a superb replica of Géricault's painting of a Chasseur of the French Imperial Guard*

Following pages: An angle of a British square at Waterloo, showing the Royal Horse Artillery. Diorama created by Derek Cross

Below: This diorama with General Ulysses Grant at Vicksburg during the American Civil War is in the Testi Collection although the figures may be Britain *adaptations*

Ney, Kutuzov, Rommel, Wolfe, Washington, Grant, Moltke—the list of figures on the market could keep you busy for a long time.

Two of the most popular periods for collectors are the Napoleonic Wars and the armies of Frederick the Great in the Seven Years War. There is tremendous variety of uniform in both these major conflicts. For example, Germany was divided into about 300 different states up until Napoleonic times. Some of these states had armies of only a handful of men but they still had their own characteristic uniform. Napoleon swept most of the states away but even up to 1914 there were still 26 independent German states. The Bavarians, for instance, had quite different uniforms to the Prussians, and any Prussian soldiers on manoeuvres were not allowed to enter Bavarian territory without specific permission.

The richness of Napoleonic uniform is not the only reason for its popularity. France itself is considered to be the cradle of the collector. Many of the earliest model soldiers were Napoleonic, reflecting the period of France's greatest glory. The regiments of Imperial Guards, the names of the battlegrounds on which the French armies fought—Austerlitz, Jena, Borodino—the name of the Emperor himself: all these are rich historical memories.

The Germans favour the period of Frederick the Great because that, too, was a time of great variety in uniform and a peak of Prussian glory. The importance of Germany in the development of model soldiers has ensured that the popularity of this period has spread all over the world. Once again, the name of Frederick himself, the might of military Prussia, battles such as Leuthen and Rossbach still send echoes down through the centuries. As in the Napoleonic Wars, the Seven Years War was a conflict of many nations, in which Austria, France, Russia, Saxony and Sweden all attempted to contain the expansionist ambitions of Prussia.

Britain was about the only power to stand beside Frederick during that upheaval. Today in Britain, collectors buy French and Prussian figures but the main emphasis is on the British Army itself up to 1914. World War II is steadily becoming increasingly popular but, strangely enough, the greater interest lies with the German troops. *Tradition* sell 20 German figures of World War II for every one British soldier. Roy Belmont-Maitland has found over the years that whatever period people collect they almost invariably collect the losing side. French Napoleonic figures are more popular than British Napoleonic; the Confederate Army of the American Civil War is more popular than the Union Army.

Having decided what period to collect you must now decide on the size. The widest range is in the standard 54-mm size. You may prefer the larger available dimensions, such as 77-mm, 80-mm or 90-mm which for some people may be easier to paint. The 90-mm is a comparatively new scale and offers less scope. You may prefer figures in the smaller 25-mm size, which can still have an astonishing amount of detail. Your choice will depend on how much you want to pay, how much room you have and how you want to display your collection.

A spare room is obviously the ideal place to lay out the collection, using tables, shelves, and even the floor. Not everyone, however, will have that amount of space. A display case or book case is probably the easiest way to keep the figures and show them off to permanent advantage. Open shelves can be used and painted so that they act as a natural background and base for the figures. Or you can use wooden boxes on their sides, to make your own display cases. In the section of this book on dioramas, you will find some advice on how to build up the scenery for a group that you might want to put on permanent show.

There are several magnificent displays of model soldiers still in existence, even though the age of the great collectors is past. We have already mentioned the collections of paper soldiers in Paris, Naples and Madrid. In Italy there is the Testi Collection near Padua and the collection of Count

Vitteti. In France there are still a few wealthy private collectors. There is a collection at West Point in America but there are no big national collections. One of the largest collections of military books and prints is owned by Brown University in Rhode Island.

There are museums with collections in Leipzig, Cologne, Compiègne and Dover. There are several private collectors in Britain; Switzerland already has collections and the Japanese and Australians are becoming collectors. If you want to know where your nearest public collection is, your best move is probably to contact a local museum or even a nearby army unit, since many regiments have their own collections.

Above: 17th Light Dragoon under Sir Banastre Tarleton's command during the American War of Independence. This is an Imrie-Risley figure

Opposite page: A detachment of Cuirassiers during the march past for Kaiser Wilhelm II in Berlin on the eve of World War I. These figures are in the Testi Collection

Wargames

Wargames have a history as old as chess. With miniature soldiers, you can refight the world's great battles and, by following the strictest rules of possibility, change a classic defeat into an outstanding victory

Above: An amphibious landing during the opening stages of a wargame. Such landings make enjoyable wargames, particularly the Allied landing at Anzio in 1944 when the Germans were taken completely by surprise before they counter-attacked with vigour. The detail in this layout makes it a permanent and attractive display as well

The wargame is an elaborate extension of the ancient military exercise of chess. It is also another very satisfactory approach to collecting military miniatures, in as much as they are made use of instead of just being looked at. For reasons of cost and convenience, wargamers use the smaller figures of 25 mm and less. Often they collect thousands of them so that they can represent a battle in a ratio of something like one model soldier for every three or four soldiers present in the original battle.

There are two quite different ways of playing. You can recreate a particular battle and stick faithfully to the order of events, laying your pieces out on a large table-top and meticulously following the manoeuvres of the historical occasion until you reach the historical outcome. Or you can commence with the historical battle order and then, with dice and cards, contest your own outcome, so that Rommel might win Alamein, Napoleon might win Waterloo, or Hannibal might win Zama.

The second method is only partly a game of chance. Factual accuracy is fundamentally important and modifies the casual throw of the dice. The game usually begins with the soldiers and their equipment set out in accordance with the opening of the battle. Dice are then thrown to determine their subsequent moves, each throw involving a great many complex manoeuvres.

Strict rules are laid down for the distances that regiments and troops may move. But a throw of the dice may decide the effect of a cannon ball; it might decide just how demoralizing has been the effect of the death of a staff officer or the capture of the commissariat. There are rules which must be worked out to decide how many moves can be made by a soldier before he needs to eat or sleep, or how far a tank can travel before it needs to refuel. In these resting periods the next chance to move is missed. Soldiers and vehicles in groups must move more slowly than when single and similarly hilly terrain must be covered more slowly than open ground. Every possible effect of a real situation is incorporated into the game so that a realistic outcome can be achieved.

Fortunate or deplorable changes in the weather are usually taken into account before play begins, according to the meteorological facts of history. A sudden change in the weather can alter the course of a whole engagement. In real life, a downpour won the battle of Plassey for Clive of India since the French failed to cover their gunpowder. As a result the French and Indian forces of 50,000 were routed by the East India Company's 3,200 men and 10 guns, with gunpowder that had been carefully protected by tarpaulins.

Wargames provide an excellent way for people to work out their enthusiasm with others. There are many clubs where games are played that last the whole week-end or longer. The same battle can be fought many times with a different outcome every game. Wargames also provide an outlet for the hobby instinct; the ground can be built up to a replica of the original battle site, with model houses, trees, water, ravines, shell holes and hills. This puts the figures on permanent display—a display that can turn to furious action once the dice begin to roll.

In the mid-nineteenth century the wargame, or *Kriegspiel* as it was known, was regarded as an important aspect of German military training. Experimental tactics were tested and the effects of cavalry and infantry manoeuvres carefully gauged against the response of the enemy. Young officers became used to controlling the movement of substantial numbers of troops in battle. Surprisingly, when the wargame came to Britain, it came in a non-military form; it was introduced as

a game by the writer H. G. Wells, whose book *Little Wars* remains a classic.

The type of battle you choose to set up for your wargame will largely depend on the period of figures you favour. It may also depend on the number of figures you have or mean to collect and what kind of ratio of figures to soldiers you can hope for. Some wargames are now played on a skirmish basis, man for man, using 54-mm figures. At the battle of Marathon, in 491 BC, the Greeks defeated the Persians with 11,000 soldiers to their 15,000. Those were relatively small armies and you might well aim for a three-to-one or four-to-one ratio. Alexander the Great, 160 years later, confronted far larger Persian forces at the Battle of Issus; his 30,000 men faced a Persian army of 100,000 and lost about 450 soldiers against Persian losses of 50,000. A wargame might well produce a very different outcome.

The Battle of Bunker Hill during the American War of Independence provides a smaller scale engagement than Marathon. While 15,000 troops from Massachusetts, Connecticut, Rhode Island and New Hampshire were assembled to hem in the 5,000 men stationed in Boston under General Gage, a small but vital struggle took place outside the town for control of the hills that offered a good field of artillery fire over the town. Colonel Prescott of Massachusetts, with about 1,000 men, dug in on the top of Bunker's Hill and a detachment of 2,300 troops under Major-General Howe were sent out by Gage to dislodge them. Although the British forced the New Englanders to withdraw, both sides suffered severe losses, which demoralized the British and gave the New Englanders renewed confidence as they believed the odds against them were not insuperable. Washington took command of the American troops a few weeks later and moulded them into an organized force which was able to compel the British to evacuate the town.

Generally, however, the average size of most armies steadily increased over the centuries. In eighteenth-century Europe Frederick the Great's armies averaged about 40,000. The armies of the Thirty Years War, 100 years earlier, averaged half that number. Napoleon's armies at the beginning of the nineteenth century averaged 90,000 men. In World War I the combined German forces numbered about 1,500,000 on each of the two fronts, East and West.

The number of dead in modern warfare is often greater than the total of those involved in many early conflicts. The massed dead of Antietam in the American Civil War and the slaughter of the Russo-Japanese War were appalling sights. In one day in July 1916, the British alone lost more than 57,000 men on a single battlefield in Europe. But there is no need for the wargamer to complain that he has been landed with the losing side. There may be no need for him to sacrifice his men. Wargames can have some very surprising results, results to warm the heart of many an old soldier.

Research

Miniature soldiers are fascinating for the detail of their uniforms and their colouring. Getting this detail right will lead you to national and regimental museums, art galleries, photograph albums, old prints, personal memoirs—an intriguing world to research with new interest

Choosing a battle to suit your models and finding out the numbers involved in that battle are just two elements in the research which can be the most engrossing pursuit involved in collecting model soldiers. The word 'research' is a little heavy for a pleasure that you will quickly regard as a thoroughly enjoyable indulgence. Points of reference will be old uniforms, prints, pictures, history books, diaries, military museums, weapons, photographs and even topographical studies of the nature of the ground on which your battles were fought.

If you are going to go to the expense and effort of buying model soldiers, assembling, painting and converting them, then you are going to want details to be correct. The master-craftsman makes sure that he supplies you with a figure that has every buckle, button and sash appropriate to it. It is up to you to make sure that such details are not lost when you start painting the figure.

It is unlikely that you are starting without any knowledge of history at all. If you decide that you would like to have a 'redcoat' British soldier or a Confederate 'rebel' or a Nazi stormtrooper, the chances are that they have taken your fancy because you know something about that period of history. You might then want to learn a little bit more about the troops on the other side or maybe you will want to extend your range to other periods. But, it is difficult to know which period to choose, so you might turn to the history books.

Above left. The splendid uniforms of these turcos or native soldiers of the French colonial army in Algeria were copied by certain units in the American Civil War but proved quite impractical and were soon dropped

Above: Museums are excellent sources for original research. This portrait of a sepoy or native cavalryman of the British East India Company hangs in the Victoria and Albert Museum in London

Far left: However romanticized historical prints of military subjects may sometimes be, they still remain excellent reference for uniform detail. This ornate garb is worn by Major-General Sir Augustus Frazer of the Royal Horse Artillery during the Napoleonic Wars

Research

Military history is not the tedious schoolbook history of statutes, papal bulls, economic policies or parliamentary debates. It is history full of colour, liveliness, excitement and humour. Books may be useful for research but other helpful sources are art galleries and army museums, as well as personal records and photograph albums. Most libraries will have some material you can use.

The best way to begin researching is to jot down everything you learn, either in a card index or a scrapbook. A scrapbook reference library is invaluable. Look for old prints and details of uniforms in historical magazines, old books, or even reliable modern books. Tear out what you want and paste it up according to your own

Right: This painting is in the collection of the National Army Museum, London. The schapka *head-dress which the officer of the 23rd Light Dragoons (Lancers) is holding was originally of Polish design*

Far right: The original of this painting can be found in the India Office Library, London. Here British troops attack the Sikh Army at Moodkee in 1845

Below: Also in the National Army Museum, London, this painting provides good reference for British general and staff officers, 1865–1870

method in a scrapbook, as Roy Belmont-Maitland has done. This method has given him an extensive reference library which is second to none.

He is one of a handful of people who buy every book and magazine on military uniforms that is produced. He cuts out the information he wants and pastes it into his own carefully ordered scrapbooks so that his library is organized to his own shape and system. He can tell you the uniform of a Romanian dragoon officer of 1850 within .two minutes.

There are many books on modelling and on uniforms, some of which are excellent but you should always be cautious. Many of the books are rehashes of other books which may not always have been thoroughly researched. Mistakes are perpetuated because the books are produced in too much of a hurry. There is only one way of finding out whether a book is reliable and that is by going back to the original source and checking. Visit a military museum or a national museum or a print gallery and check one or two of the uniforms in the book against an original print or, better still, the original uniform.

This 'original' research is a good idea anyway. Even a local public library may well have some old books stored away which have some contemporary prints of uniforms in them. Books of prints in antique shops can be expensive today and many of them have already been bought by collectors but there is always time to snatch a quick glance

at some detail if you come across a book appropriate to your period.

The best form of research is tracking down the original uniform itself so that you can feel its texture and gain absolute confidence in the authenticity of your model. Regimental museums can sometimes help as well as national museums such as, in Britain, the Victoria and Albert Museum, the British Museum, the National Army Museum, the Imperial War Museum and Edinburgh Castle. In America the Smithsonian Institution and the Museum of the United States Military Academy at West Point can also be of help, as can the Army Museums in Brussels, Leyden, and Madrid, Les Invalides in Paris and newly started German museums in Rastadt and Bavaria.

Be careful, however, that in your search for the exact colours of a uniform you do not expect every uniform to be precisely the same. Make allowances for the dyes of the period, which often varied in shading and led to quite considerable differences in uniforms that were all meant to be the same— even the experts disagree on some details. For example, the orders for uniform may stipulate a certain style whereas in practice regulation dress may never have been worn, either because it was unavailable or too impractical. On the other hand certain styles may have been worn that never had official sanction. If you really intend to get it right it is always best to refer to two sources and see if they agree.

39

Some of the best sources are the paintings and photographs executed by painters and photographers who were officially attached to the army or who were actually engaged in the battle. The Battles of Borodino and Marengo in the Napoleonic Wars were painted by General Baron Lejeune and are excellent sources of detailed information about the uniforms of that period. Many of his paintings are in the Palace of Versailles. More recently the photographs of Brady provide a lot of first-hand information about the American Civil War. In France and Germany sets of postcards and uniform sheets can be bought in addition to your reference collection, these are usually fairly accurate, but they are not readily available in other countries. So if you know anyone who is living or travelling abroad, you could ask them to collect some.

As your knowledge and reference builds up you will find yourself coming across intriguing pieces of information. You might discover a uniform so small that you think it is a child's fancy dress. Roy Belmont-Maitland has just such a uniform which belonged to a British officer of a Shropshire Yeomanry Regiment of 1809. The officer was a boy of twelve. His voice would barely have broken.

You will begin to get acquainted with a strange new vocabulary, and the various parts of the uniform will soon trip lightly off your tongue. You

may know what a busby and a bearskin are but do you know that an aiguillette is the plaited cord worn over the shoulder? Here are some other useful terms: a shoulder ornament is called an epaulette; a pelisse was a short cloak or mantle worn slung over one shoulder and a shabraque was a saddlecloth. The armour worn around the neck and retained symbolically by certain officers long after its medieval use had faded was called a gorget. Do you know that the breastplate and backplate still worn by British Lifeguards is called a cuirass?

You will quickly learn to distinguish a grenadier from a dragoon, or a fusilier from a hussar. The fusilier got his name from the lightweight 'fusil' or musket that he carried in the seventeenth century. The smartly adorned hussar with the fur-edged pelisse was descended from the Hungarian light cavalry. The dragoon was an infantry soldier capable of riding to battle but expected to fight on foot. The grenadier, not unnaturally, was once armed with a grenade. In time the title was retained as a mark of honour to differentiate grenadiers from ordinary infantrymen. They became an elite company of the tallest soldiers in the army.

Uniforms became symbols of fashion, this is seen clearly in the case of the Hungarians who influenced the hussars of many nations. Other regiments were influenced by the dashing Cossacks. French fashion of the First and Second Empire made itself felt all over Europe in the nineteenth century. As much as anything, soldiers were anxious to try out the effect of the latest military styles on the ladies of the town, however impractically tight or uncomfortable those styles might be in practice.

New styles in head-dresses flooded through Europe, from the shako to the kepi, until the German pickelhaube firmly put a spike on the practical hard helmet of militarism. The cut-away tailcoat was replaced by the tunic. Khaki spread from the army in India to the armies of all the combatants during World War I. After 1918, the old splendour was relegated to parade dress only. Gone were the days when the love of tradition and the taste of your tailor determined the idiosyncracies of uniform. Gone were the days when Lord Cardigan of the Light Brigade had his own men's uniforms made by a West End tailor.

Every period has its own characteristics. If you are interested in medieval knights you will find yourself surrounded by the symbols of heraldry. Crests, bar sinisters and escutcheons will crowd your mind. You may well visit colleges of arms or churches and cathedrals where the arms of fourteenth and fifteenth century knights may be displayed on their tombs.

If it is the seventeenth or eighteenth centuries that attract you, you will find it helpful to know something about the hairstyles of soldiers and officers. You will learn about the queuing of hair and about wigs. You will discover the difference between the powder used on the hair of an officer and the tallow and flour used by the rank and file.

Whatever period you favour, you will need to understand both the anatomy and the way of life of the soldiers of the time: the bow legs of the Scythian and Mongol horsemen; the rough peasants and motley-dressed townsmen of Washington's army or the even rougher peasants of the blind Jan Žižká's Hussite army; the clean face of an officer accustomed to a leisured life in contrast to the bucolic face of the farmhand corporal or the sallowness of the enforced recruit. You will soon be able to distinguish an Apache from a Huron, the stature of a Roman from that of a Goth or a Celt or a Pict and that of a Vietnamese from that of a U.S. Marine.

The various stages in the development of handguns and cannon represents another fascinating field of knowledge. There are prints of knights in armour with guns or 'dogs' slung round their necks. The extensive armoury of the Emperor Maximilian is recorded in ornately illustrated catalogues. You might have to learn to distinguish a matchlock from an arquebus, a wheel-lock musket from a wheel-lock carbine, a flint-lock from a percussion, a Dreyse needlegun from a French chassepôt, a Brown Bess from a Kentucky rifle. The Gatling of the American Civil War, the

Far left: Print from the collection of Colonel J. B. R. Nicholson, showing in excellent detail the uniforms of French Officers of the Bourbon Restoration, 1814–1815. From left to right, two Gendarmes du Roi, a Grey Musketeer in undress, a dragoon officer and a Grey Musketeer in full dress

Below: This painting shows the sash of General Kléber, commander of the French Army in Egypt, 1799

41

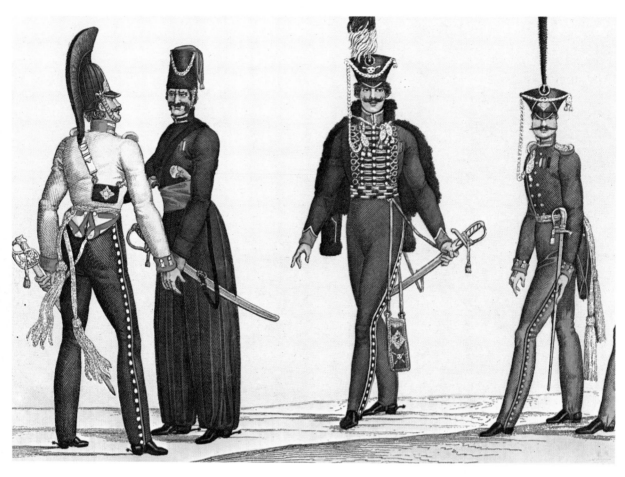

French Mitrailleuse, the Browning and the Maxim are all machine guns which were characteristic of their period. Military hardware from tanks to troop-carriers, from culverins to the dreaded German 88-mm may become part of your collection and it is useful to know their national peculiarities.

The nature of supplies, camps and tents are all interesting bits of additional information. Even the manner of sword and rifle drill is important. For example, it helps to know how a seventeenth century musketeer shouldered his musket; how he gave fire; how he poised his musket, trailed his rest, cocked his match, drew forth his scouring stick and rammed home. You may know what a goose-step looks like but do you know how other armies marched in procession or stood at ease? If you do not, you may animate the limbs of your figures completely wrongly.

Mounted bowmen and cavalry require special knowledge. The Assyrians, Phrygians, Scythians, Macedonians and Romans all used mounted horsemen but had no stirrups and no proper saddles. The stirrup was not used widely in Europe until the eighth century. It enabled the knight to stand up in his saddle and withstand the shock of another's lance. Two centuries earlier the saddle had been used by the Byzantine and Persian armies at the time of the remarkable Byzantine general Belisarius. The sixth-century cataphracts, as the knights were called, were

Above: Contemporary paintings were not always flattering but nonetheless this French painting of officers of the Prussian army of occupation in Paris in 1815 provides authentic reference for their uniforms

Above right: A useful parade of officers and men of the Prussian guards cavalry regiments, 1871, from the collection of Lt-Colonel J. B. R. Nicholson. From left to right—staff officer of Guards Cuirassiers; lieutenant of the Garde du Corps in full dress; trooper of Black Cuirassiers; lieutenant of Guards Lancers; trooper of Guards Lancers in parade dress; trumpeter of Guards Dragoons in parade dress; lieutenant of Life Guard Hussars; staff trumpeter in winter uniform

Right: Variations in cavalry uniforms from the Kingdom of Saxony, 1871. From left to right—lieutenant of Guards cavalry in palace uniform; trumpeter of carbineers in full dress; lancer of 2nd Ulanen, 18th Regiment, in full dress; unteroffizier of 1st Ulanen, 17th Regiment, in undress; lieutenant 2nd Hussars, 18th Regiment, in full dress; hussar in basic uniform; hussar in field dress; regimental sutler of cavalry

entirely covered in scale armour, which was laid over their horses as well. Some cataphracts had perfectly shaped metal masks that followed the contours of their face exactly.

Harness changed greatly over the centuries. Greek and Egyptian charioteers were unable to make full use of the strength of their horses because the harness was mistakenly placed around their neck and windpipe. The full strength of the horse as a working animal was not realized until the harness was placed around its shoulders. Throughout history there are also many changes in the style of bit—another field for research if you are going to concentrate on mounted figures.

The wargamer will probably study the tactics and strategy of the greatest military thinkers: the Greek hoplite order of battle in straight lines, in contrast to Frederick the Great's 'oblique order' in angled lines; the star-shaped forts and siege techniques of the seventeenth century Frenchman Sebastien de Vauban; the military philosophies of Maurice de Saxe, who fought for the French at Malplaquet when he was only thirteen; the writings of the Roman Vegetius or the Dutch lawyer Edward Grotius who first tried to codify international rules of war in a book called *On the law of War and Peace* in 1625. In modern times the tank philosophy of J. F. C. Fuller could give the wargamer many new ideas for tactical and strategic manoeuvres to enliven his game.

All this wealth of material and background detail may seem a little overwhelming at first glance. But, it is here to give you a glimpse of how much there is to learn and enjoy and what a vast field of endless interest you can approach. Do not worry if it all seems overwhelming. You can buy your model ready painted from the shop and admire it all the same. Or you can follow the painting instructions in simple steps to give yourself a feeling of achievement. That achievement and sense of pleasure will not be any the less merely because you do not know what the soldier had to eat on the eve of the battle in which you imagine he took part.

Much of the information you might casually dig up is best thought of as a source of inspiration. It is difficult to resist the bright colours and outlandish names that give a lift to the spirit of adventure. The dashing light blue of an officer of the Bercheny Hussars of Louis XVI's cavalry contrasts with the yellow of the Saxon cuirassiers of the time of Frederick the Great. The red and blue of the Dromedary regiment of the French Army in Egypt before the First Empire contrasts strongly with the outlandish costume of a Mameluke of Napoleon's Imperial Guard. There are many fascinating differences of detail between the medieval-looking Tcherkess horsemen and the green-coated Bashkir horsemen of the Russian Army that tried to stop Napoleon's advance to Moscow.

The names and details of hundreds of regiments evoke alien lands and brave encounters throughout the world: the grey uniform of a Mecklenberg

musketeer of 1839; a Prussian Uhlan of 1821, in dark blue and grey, armed with a lance; one of Garibaldi's red-shirts; the blue of the American cavalry; the red and blue of the French Foreign Legion; the yellow turbans of the renowned Skinner's Horse of the British Army; the feathered hat of the Italian Bersaglieri of 1890; the pitchfork bayonet of the Chinese army of 1880. You may believe you know what troops of the two World Wars looked like but have you come across a French Spahi on horseback or a Tirailleur Indochinois? Do you know what a German Uhlan of the Macedonian Front wore, and can you recognize the uniform of the army of Montenegro, or of a Pomeranian artilleryman of 1890?

Left: Contemporary illustration of the British hussar uniform at its most elaborate, from the collection of Lt-Colonel J. B. R. Nicholson. This is an officer of the 10th Hussars, 1854

Below left: Print from the Mansell Collection, London, showing a group of Russian cavalry and infantry officers, 1815

Below: French influence shows clearly in the uniforms of these infantry of the army of Italy during the Napoleonic Wars; in a print from the collection of Lt-Colonel J. B. R. Nicholson

Farther back in history there are still more names that crowd the mind with images and stories. There are Greek hoplites, Roman aquilifers, Praetorian guards. There are soldiers from Islam who swept into Spain and challenged the knights of Charlemagne. The mitred helmets of medieval bishops at war intermingle with Burgundian, Tyrolean and Templar knights. The colours of English infantry of the fourteenth century serving with private families are multifarious. The jerkins of the Welsh longbowmen contrast with the partial armour of the Genoese crossbowmen. The sixteenth century is full of idiosyncratic costumes: the green suit of the German Hurenwebel, the wide armour skirt of the Feldhauptmann, the bright, flamboyant costumes of the Swiss and German Landsknechts. Beefeaters and Janissaries; Incas, Aztecs and Mayas; the armoured Samurai and the Minamoto soldiers of fourteenth- and fifteenth-century Japan; the halberdiers of the Brussels civic guard—these are only a very few of the uniforms and soldiers that span man's violent and fascinating history.

The field stretches more than 5,000 years back to the first depicted soldiers, which are seen on the Royal Standard of Ur. It takes in the Bayeux Tapestry and concludes in twentieth-century Malaya, Korea, Vietnam and the Middle East. Once your interest is caught you are assured of inexhaustible material, and no doubt you will be constantly on the alert.

The Russian guns engaged with the Light Brigade at the Battle of Balaclava, 1854. This is another view of the diorama shown on the cover of this book

Materials

Here are some simple and useful hints to start you off with the right materials and tell you how to make the best use of the tools of the trade. Master the elementary techniques and you will have no trouble with any of the later projects

Alan Caton firmly regards his paints and paint-brushes as the most useful pieces of equipment he has for working with model soldiers. With them he can put the finer detail on his figures. He can transform a uniform from one nationality to another; he can change the rank and regiment of a soldier; he can bring a well-sculpted piece of metal to life.

Care of the brushes is most important. There is much truth in the saying that a good workman values what he works with. There are many kinds of fine paintbrushes available. Alan uses Red Sables Numbers One and Two, with a Number One cut down for fine detail. You will see how to cut the brush down in the drawings. Keep a spare brush for working with metallic colours such as silver and gold.

Always clean the brushes after use with white spirit or turpentine and wash them occasionally with warm, soapy water. Remake the points by rolling the tip of the brush between the lips before leaving it to dry. Only do this when you have already washed the brush.

There are several kinds of suitable paint. The best are basically oil-based plastic enamel paints. Of these, Humbrol paints are the most commonly available. Airfix paints are a good alternative, and Plaka paints can also be used. Acrylic paints may also be used but they are water-based and do not cover so well. Nor do they give such good detail. Another disadvantage of acrylic paints is that they dry to a dead flat finish. If you pick the figure up quite often, this will result in shiny finger prints remaining on the model. Plastic enamels are much harder and therefore better for this purpose.

Never be afraid to mix and blend gloss and matt paints for new effects. Such a mixture can provide an excellent eggshell finish for polished leather, for example. There are many interesting effects that you can obtain by experimentation. Varnish, for instance, will transform a painted surface. Winton matt varnish is a jelly-like substance which goes completely clear when heated. If you brush this over a horse that has been painted in dead flat colours, the horse will take on a slightly shiny, freshly groomed appearance.

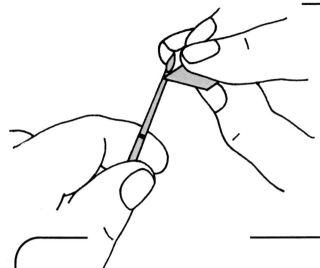

You will often need to have a paintbrush that has been cut down for fine detail. To cut the brush, rotate the base of the bristles against a sharp blade, shaving off the outer layers of the brush until you are left with a very fine, long springy point. A number one brush is best for this.

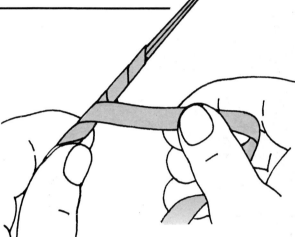

Some tools have a handle that is much too far from the point to enable you to exert proper finger-tip control. Your fingers need to be close to the point of contact with the work. To solve this problem, hold the shaft of the tool and wind elastic bands or insulating tape around the shaft; this will protect your hands when you are working.

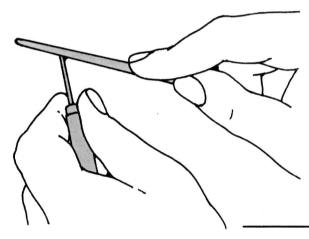

You can make your own tools by filing down those available in the shops. A screwdriver ground down to a fine edge can make a useful little chisel. An x-shaped screwdriver filed down can make an excellent gouge for uniform creases and working around the ears. Several different shapes of tip can be achieved by working on this type of screwdriver.

Left: The superbly painted figure of Prince Carl of Prussia as Colonel-in-Chief of the 15th Uhlans

Right: You will need to collect a wide range of colours for some of the elaborate uniforms of the past, and a variety of brushes for painting

Experiment with your paints as well. When you first use a colour, always test it on a palette of some kind, even if this is only a piece of cardboard or an old tin lid. Try mixing your colours to make new colours. Note the subtle differences between using a lighter shade of one colour or lightening the shade of the original colour by adding white. Such differences may well determine the authenticity of a uniform. Colouring demands the most exact research into detail, and here good colour reference pictures are essential.

There are certain basic tools you will need for actually shaping the metal and for building up the solid structure of the figures. Of these a soldering iron is probably the most formidable to someone who has not handled one before. But if you follow the instructions on the opposite page you should quickly learn how to use the iron. You will probably need two soldering irons—a heavy 65 watt iron for the main work and a lighter 25 or 30 watt iron for accessories such as firearms. You will use the iron for joining heads and limbs and for adding metal to the figure to build up clothes and equipment.

After soldering you must add detail and finesse to the joins you have made. For this work you will need files, knives and punches. Provide yourself with as good a supply of files as you can obtain. All shapes will be useful: flat files, round files, half-round files, triangular files, square files, mouse-tailed files. You can also make your own

Below: A selection of useful tools for working with model soldiers and making conversions.

1   *Files of various shapes*
2   *Modeller's saw*
3   *Tin snips or metal shears*
4   *Pair of pliers*
5   *Craft knife*
6   *65 watt soldering iron*
7   *25 watt soldering iron*
8   *Engraving tool, diamond section*
9   *Engraving tool, chisel blade*
10   *Converted screwdriver, as chisel*
11   *Hollow-nosed punch*
12   *Soldering fluid*
13   *Solder*

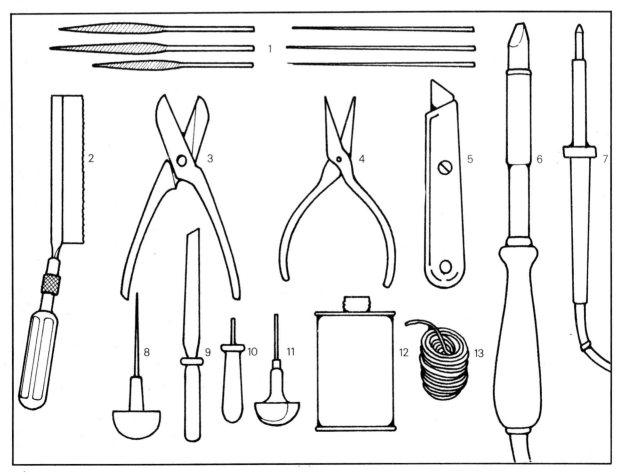

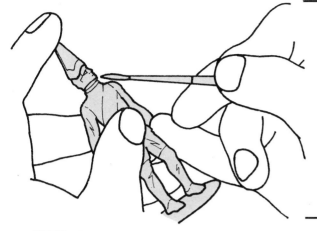

Soldering can be used to join two pieces of metal together. Here we show how to join a head to a body. The process is the same for joining limbs or any other part of a figure. First trim the bits of metal to be joined and heat up the iron in preparation. Hold the body and the head in one hand so that they are touching at the desired angle. Apply soldering fluid to both surfaces with an old paintbrush.

The fluid helps the solder to run onto the metal. Dip the iron into the fluid and then onto the solder. You will find that you can pick up a bit of solder on the end of the iron. For figures larger than 54 mm, you must use a large iron or the heat will be insufficient. When you come to apply the solder to the figure, the heat of a smaller iron would dissipate into the figure and the solder would not run properly.

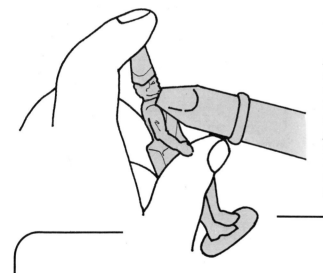

Apply the iron to the join of the body and head. Touch it to the join quickly and then take the iron away at once. The solder will flow from the iron over the surfaces. It will solidify almost immediately to join the two parts. Be careful, if you are doing quite a bit of soldering on the figure, as the metal will heat up and become uncomfortable to hold. Keep your fingers well away from the tip of the iron and the molten solder.

Once you have joined the head and body, fill in the remaining gap of the neck with more solder. Make sure that the surfaces are well coated with fluid and always dip your iron into the fluid before picking up the next bit of solder. Build up the gap bit by bit with the solder and then use a file to establish the final shape.

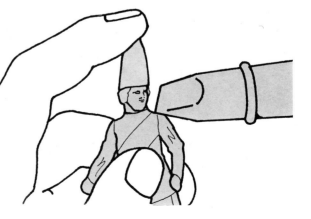

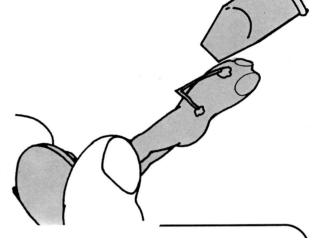

Solder can also be used to build up new pieces of equipment and add material to a uniform. All that you need to do is to make a wire frame, fix the frame to the figure and then fill the frame with solder. Here we show you how to add a coat to a figure that has been filed down. Attach a wire frame to the front of the figure with a blob of solder at the points where the frame touches the figure.

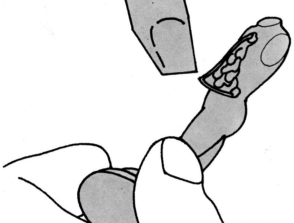

The coat stands away from the figure at the bottom end, so be careful to build up the solder a very little at a time, so that a gap is left between body and coat. In this diagram only the last blob remains to be added. Surface tension will cause it to spread, like a soap bubble between the hands, and solidify immediately without dropping through to the body. This wire frame method can also be used for making rifles, holsters, hats, packs and so on.

snapes from other tools by filing them down to your particular requirements.

A craft knife is also essential, equipped with heavy-duty blades. You will need this knife to pare away the metal before finishing off the detail with the file.

A hollow-nosed punch saves a lot of trouble with buttons. As the name implies, this simple metal rod has a hollow nose which can be pressed against the uniform of the figure on which you are working to leave the impression of a button. When you are working on uniforms that are ornately decorated with buttons, this can greatly cut down time and effort.

Engraving tools are helpful but not essential. These can act as scoops or chisels to cut into the finer detail of the figure. You can make your own engraving tools from other tools.

Once you start working on model soldiers you will probably find that you acquire one or two engraving tools for certain specialist tasks. Particular angles of the blade will be especially useful for shaping details such as ears, mouths, fingers and noses, as well as lapels, collars and cuffs, the buckles on belts, the tops of boots, and the delicate detail of helmets.

For tougher work you will need a pair of metal cutters or tin snips. These should be strong enough to cut accessories such as weapons and wire, as well as being able to cut through anything as thick as the wrist or even the arm or neck of the

figure. You will need a modelling saw for cutting through thicker lead or perhaps even a proper hacksaw. For this kind of work you will also need a small vice which you can clamp to your workbench. Never be afraid to go to work on your figures fairly roughly in the first instance if you intend to make dramatic changes. You can always work the final detail in later.

A small hammer will be useful, for hammering a piece of metal flat. You will certainly need it for making dioramas where you will have to nail bits of wood together. A pair of pliers is also essential. There are round-nosed and thin-nosed types and you will probably find a use for both.

You may even need some drills for making holes in the metal of a figure. There is an example in the trooper of Custer's last stand which Alan Caton has recreated as one of the complex conversions later in this book. Holes have been drilled into the trooper's back so that the arrows embedded in him can be fixed more securely.

There are various kinds of drill available. There are hand-held and hand-powered drills, which also go under the name of pin-drills or rotary drills. There are power drills especially made for modellers, which can be driven either by batteries or by mains electricity. Or there are dentists' drills. These are primarily heavy-duty drills for making your own tools. A hand-powered drill will probably be sufficient at first.

You will find your own natural way to hold the

tools. On page 49 we show you how to wrap rubber bands or tape around the shaft of an engraving tool so that you can get a grip closer to the point, which will give you greater control over your work.

Another trick to give you closer control over the sharp edge of an engraving tool is to slip the empty ink-container of a ballpoint pen over the tool to protect your fingers. This is a great help, particularly when you have to apply a certain amount of pressure.

Various adhesives can be used. There are those which are ideal for making quick joins because they grip almost instantly. Others act as fillers. Plastic padding is also very useful for securing figures firmly to a base and providing certain effects for water.

There are many different materials readily available in your home that you will find useful. Pipe cleaners can be used for plumes. Old photograph negatives can be cut down for straps and reins for horses. Embroidery cottons and silks can be braided together for aiguillettes and epaulettes.

Tea bags have endless uses. The tea itself makes ideal groundwork beneath a tree or can even be used for the leaves of the tree. The bag can be used as camouflage for artillery. Corks can be cut into rock shapes.

Ballpoint pen refills make excellent glasses when cut to length. Lollipop sticks cut to make

Above: Never throw away any bits you cut from a figure. A bits box can be a treasure trove when you want a spare head or a hand, a limb, a torso, a rifle or a helmet. A hunt through the bits box may give you inspiration for a new figure or a challenging conversion

Following pages: British square from the Battle of Waterloo, 1815. This is another part of the diorama also shown on pages 30 and 31. Diorama created by Derek Cross

square ends provide planks. Drinking straws can be transformed into drainpipes, toothpicks into small fences and logs of wood, split peas into small rocks or water-smoothed boulders. Aquarium gravel or birdseed can also be used for groundcover. Moss makes shrubs, herbs make larger bushes, fuse wire can be twisted into trees and used for the framework of accessories on figures.

More exotically, nylon tights when stretched make superb camouflage netting. Thin sticks of pasta make excellent bamboo shafts. Tobacco can be used for all kinds of groundcover, and is particularly good for soiled straw in stables. More commonly, any scene can be littered with bits of paper. Put your imagination to work and start looking around your own home with an eye to the possibilities of using various everyday products.

Making up a Kit

Model soldiers in kit form can be bought almost everywhere now. Some of the kits can be very complex, some are quite simple like the two we show here. But they all give the beginner and the experienced a sense of achievement

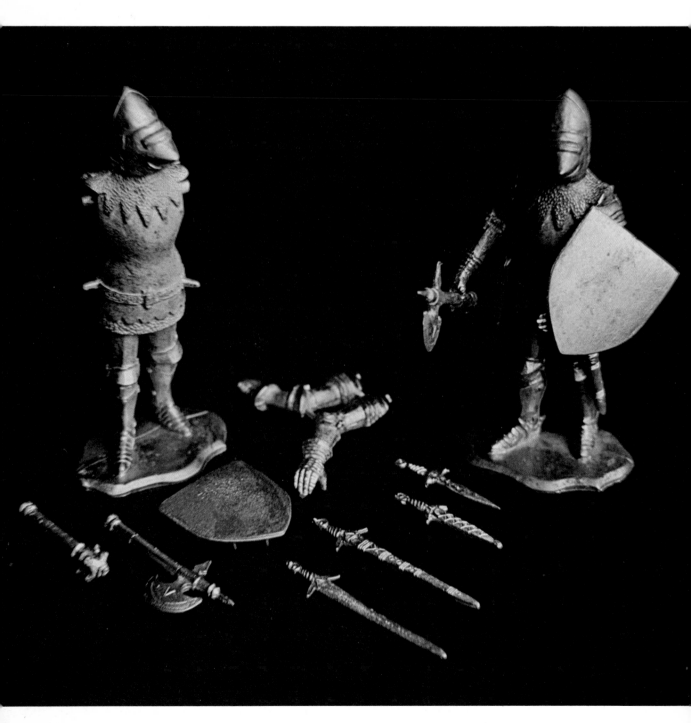

When you have cleaned off the flash and sprue, have a dry run to check that the pieces fit flush. Fit the arms first. The pieces are pegged to fit in one position, although you can make slight changes of angle. Apply adhesive and hold till dry, or use elastic bands to hold the arms to the body.

When the arms are stuck fast, fit the shield to the left arm. There are lugs on the back of the shield. Apply adhesive to the arm or to the shield and fit the shield with the lugs on either side of the arm. Bend the lugs with the pliers to grip the arm.

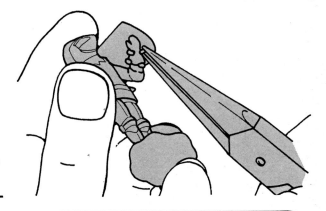

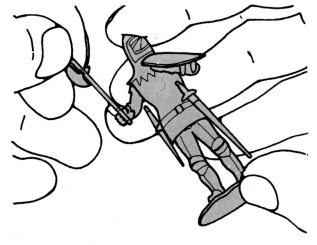

Choose the accessories you want and glue in place. We have attached the sheathed sword on the left, the sheathed dagger on the right and the battle-axe in the right hand. A drawn sword, a drawn dagger and a mace are also provided. When thoroughly dry, apply a thin coat of white as undercoat. The figure is then ready to paint.

Project 1: The Duc d'Alençon

This 54-mm figure represents the Duc d'Alençon, who fought for the King of France in the Hundred Years War. To make him you will need a knife, a small file, pliers and some adhesive. Remember to be careful with the instant adhesives which take only about ten seconds to dry rock hard.

Check that you have all the pieces. The makers usually include instructions for assembly, with a list of the pieces. First remove all the extraneous pieces of metal—or flash—and separate the arms. Use the file to smooth the figure off and remove the sprue which is the passage through which the metal is poured into the mould.

Left: On the left of the picture are the parts of the kit for the Duc d'Alençon and on the right the finished figure. The lugs on the body to which to attach arms and weapons show clearly

Right: The completed figure of Kaiser Wilhelm II is ready for its undercoat of white paint

Below: The separate parts of the kit. It is always important to make sure that the parts of the kit fit together properly in a dry run before the adhesive is applied

Project 2: Kaiser Wilhelm II

Kaiser Wilhelm II of Germany is here wearing one of his favourite uniforms, the full dress of the German Guard. The Guard was roughly equivalent to the British Household Cavalry.

The Emperor presided over a Germany that was expanding its aggressive military machine with increasing urgency. Friction with France and general suspicion of Russia's plans was already sharpening Germany's appetite for war and becoming responsible for larger peacetime armies than the world had ever seen before. The sensitivity of the Austro-Hungarian Empire did not make the European situation any easier.

Wilhelm was born in 1859 and was 29 years old when he became German Emperor and King of Prussia. He trained as an army officer and ever afterwards identified himself with his military background. He much preferred to have military advisers rather than civilian diplomats around him. His impatience and determination to govern as absolute monarch led him to dismiss Bismarck from the Chancellorship in 1890—the very man who had been responsible for the unification of the German Empire. However in World War I Wilhelm virtually gave up the supreme authority to Hindenburg and Ludendorff. After the war he was exiled in Holland where he died in 1941. He was given a military funeral by Hitler.

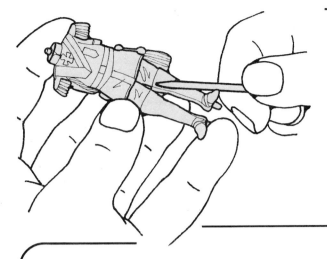

This is an 80-mm figure. Clean up the flash as shown here. A dry fit is essential as the figure is off the base. Check that there is no distortion in the legs. They are fairly malleable and can be lined up if necessary with gentle pressure.

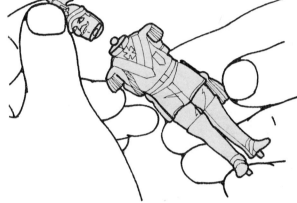

There is a peg at the neck on which to fit the head, so that the angle of the head is more or less predetermined. Only slight adjustment is possible, because the collar will also determine the angle of the head.

Fit the right hand and arm, which are in one piece, and then the left arm. Fit the left hand, with the sword and sword belt. The sword belt is very malleable. Bend it to the appropriate position against the body and fix it there with a touch of adhesive. Then fix the feet into the base, making sure that the figure is upright. Apply a thin white undercoat and paint.

General von Moltke was the Chief of Staff during World War I. The Grand Duke Nicholas took charge of the Russian forces. The French were under General Joseph Joffre and the Austro-Hungarians were under General Conrad von Hotzendorf. Lord Kitchener and General Haig were the two pre-eminent British commanders.

When the Austrian heir-apparent, the Archduke Franz Ferdinand, was assassinated at Sarajevo on 28 June 1914, the European armies had already built up to immense proportions. These armies were to be in conflict within a very short time of the declaration of war. At this time more than a million men confronted each other on both the Western and the Eastern front, quite apart from the further confrontation of forces between the Serbs and the Austro-Hungarians in the Balkans.

The number of soldiers involved by the end of World War I had greatly increased as had the number of dead which have been estimated to total anything between ten and twelve million. Of all the countries participating in the war, Germany probably fielded the largest number of enlisted people—a staggering twelve or thirteen million—even more than Russia, while the British Empire put about eight or nine million men into the war, France slightly less, Italy about five million and the United States about four million later in the war.

Painting Techniques

Painting a miniature figure is a skilful job that calls for concentration and a delicate touch. Careful and accurate research into the details of military uniforms also make it a most rewarding pastime for the hobby-enthusiast and the collector

Above: The first four stages of painting the figure of an officer in the train of Royal Artillery can be seen here from the left to the right

Project 1: A Royal Artillery Officer

The figure chosen for painting is an officer in the train of Royal Artillery in the British Army about 1690. His uniform provides an excellent opportunity to use bright scarlet, blue, crimson, orange and gold and to create a really dramatic finished work. Although the Royal Artillery were normally dressed in red coats at this time, this particular unit accompanied William of Orange to Ireland and was dressed in blue with orange facings. These were William's favourite colours and this was the only unit in the British army dressed in this fashion.

You will need about four fine brushes. One

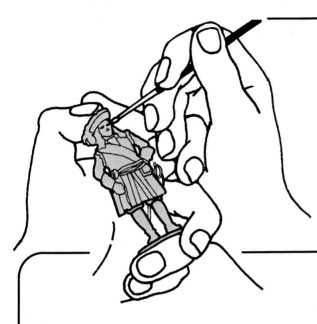

This is the best way to hold the 80-mm figure for most of the painting work. Hold the figure in the left hand (unless you are left-handed) with your thumb on top of the hat and your fingers under the base. You can swivel the figure to any angle and use the little finger of your painting hand to help steady the brush.

The right eye can sometimes be difficult to paint, particularly when it is hidden under the brim of a hat. Turn the figure upside down and you will find that you can reach it more easily. Use your little finger for extra support once more.

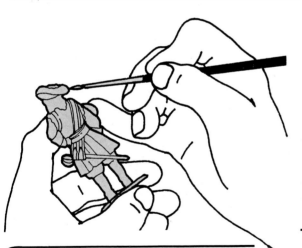

For the frills and folds such as the hat and the details of the hair hold the figure as shown. It may be easier for the beginner to stand the figure on the table to ensure that it is absolutely steady. You can get down to eye level for the finishing touches.

Stripes are easier to paint if you hold the figure sideways and draw the brush towards you, as shown here. The lines on this figure are quite short. The longer the lines, the more difficult it is to keep them parallel unless you paint them in this way. This technique is most useful for the lines of lace on a figure.

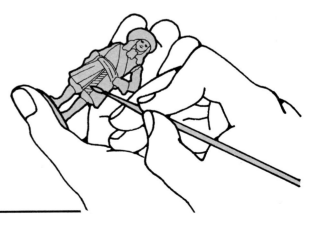

*Above: The second four stages of painting
the figure—the finished figure is on the right*

brush should be cut down for fine detail. Basic colours you will need, with the Humbrol range numbers in parenthesis, are Navy blue (HM10), British Scarlet (MC1), Black (HM6), British Crimson (MC5), Orange (MC11), Flesh (MC15), White (MC13), Hardened leather (MC27), Silver and Gold. It is better to use gold powder and gold size than gold paint out of a can, which may be expensive. There are many different tones of gold, such as pale antique and deep copper, for different types of lace. Pale antique has been used here. You will also need a bottle of white spirit or thinners.

If the figure is in kit form, first assemble the kit, clean it off with a file and undercoat with a thin coat of white paint. Leave overnight before you start further painting. Plan exactly what you are going to paint at each stage. The first four stages are shown in the picture on page 60. From left to right, they show the basic colours, the shading, the high-lighting and the metallic colours.

Paint the basic colours shown in the first figure. It is better to start with the lighter colours and work through the spectrum to the darker colours so that you are always cutting light with dark.

In the second figure shading has been added. Use a darker tone of the basic colour, rather than merely mixing black with the basic colour. Then use a clean brush barely moistened with thinner to feather the edges of the shading and blend in the

colours. Shading has been done on the coat, waist sash, gloves and waistcoat.

Use a lighter tone of the basic colour for the highlighting in the third figure. It is better not to use colours straight from the pot because of an excess of oil. Use a pallet and make your own subtle blendings of tone.

Apply the metallic colours—silver and gold—with a clean brush. These are for lace, buttons, swords and so on. Make sure your finish is as smooth as possible. Always clean the brush between colours with paint thinners and a clean rag.

Stages five to eight are shown in the colour picture on this page. The figure on the left of the row shows the addition of the features. You can see how to paint a face and how to depict some different facial expressions in the diagrams on the right-hand page. The sixth stage is to paint the hair and go over the metallic bits for definition.

In stage seven, the outlining is done. The grooves in the armour have been emphasized with a thin black line, detail has been added to the lace and the buttons have been picked out. The hat has been painted in the final figure, resting the figure on the forefinger of the supporting hand and being careful not to hold too tightly. Then the figure has been fixed to the base.

1   To paint the face, first apply overall flesh colour and then apply shading tone to eye sockets, ears, under chin, over nose and around hair and jaw lines. Then blend the edges of the shading in with a clean, slightly moist brush.

2   Paint the highlights on to the bridge of the nose, the ears, the point of the chin and on the forehead above the eyebrows. Blend the edges in and be very careful not to overdo highlighting, particularly on the nose.

3   Apply the cheek colour in the form of an inverted triangle and blend in the edges. Paint in the lips, again being careful not to produce too hard a line. With the painting of the cheeks you can really shape the face, making it gaunt or healthy.

4   Paint in the eyes and hair. The hair should be shaded and highlighted where appropriate. Add an unshaven look if you want or scars on the face. Make the hair grey at the temples for an older man.

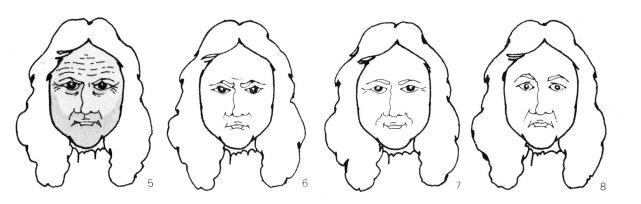

5   It is always worthwhile to add character to a face. Imagine who the figure is and what he has done. Do not be afraid to add extra detail and colour, provided you blend it in. Thin blended lines indicate an older man, for example.

6   Make the face express an emotion. For anger in a battle or duel, curve the eyebrows down in the centre and then up, as shown here. Add thin lines from the corner of the nose and the mouth but be careful not to overdo them.

7   Not every soldier looks angry or haughty. In a group scene, some of the figures may even be laughing. Add small lines around the corners of the eyes and a curved line down from the nose. Turn up the ends of the mouth and add a line.

8   Fear in battle may be a common emotion. Raise the eyebrows and paint the whites of the eyes larger and more rounded. Paint the pupil so that the white shows all round. Extend the lines down from the nose and turn the corners of the mouth down.

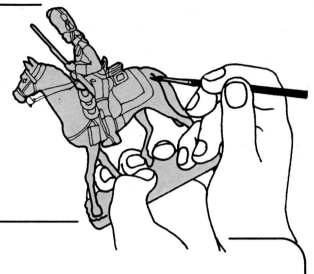

This demonstrates how best to hold a 90-mm figure on horseback. Use your fingers to brace the figure and hold it steady. Try out different hand-holds.

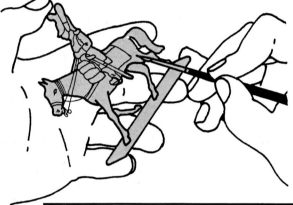

The 54-mm figure is easier to hold because it is lighter. Try this hand-hold for a start. The figure is a trumpeter of the Empress Dragoons of the French Imperial Guard at the time of Waterloo.

Project 2: Painting a Horse

It is very difficult to paint a dead flat black but even the darkest horse appears as a very, very dark brown under direct sunlight. So mix up the darkest brown you can. Use Humbrol Brown Bess (MC6) with standard black to a mix that you can still just recognize as an extremely dark brown. Apply this as the basic colour and leave to dry overnight. Then shade with pure black and highlight with Brown Bess.

Work the shading and highlighting together, pushing the colours around until you get the right shape. You must be very subtle with the tones because what you are trying to achieve is not so much shade as shape, to emphasize the bones, the hips and quarters, the muscles on the chest, the neck and so on. Run the colours smoothly together rather than in sharp lines. Think of the whole surface as a great face that needs very subtle blending of the structure of the muscles and bones beneath the skin.

Study the colour picture of the black horse on the facing page for markings that might appear on the legs and forehead. If you want an action painting of the horse in the thick of battle, use a sponge lightly tapped on to very thin white paint and dabbed gently on to the horse's chest to represent foam from the mouth. You can also have flecks of foam down the horse's flank or spatter mud on the horse in the same way.

The harness would either be black or brown. Remember that the leather would probably be well worn and highly polished. Use a half-and-half mixture of matt and gloss varnish on top of the paint to achieve a semi-gloss for the right effect.

A brown horse is much easier. Use Chestnut Brown and shade with Brown Bess. Highlight with Hardened Leather (MC27) and perhaps use black for the mane, the tail, the harness and on the legs. Use white for the other markings.

The problems in painting a grey horse are the reverse of those with a black horse. With a black horse you were shading dark with dark; with a grey horse you are highlighting white with white.

Paint the horse overall a pale grey. Shade with a darker tone of grey and highlight with pure white. The dapples on the rump have to be applied individually as carefully blended white spots.

The expression of the horse is usually shown in the cast figure. For example, if the horse is animated for combat it may have an open mouth. You can add to this by making the eyeballs look bloodshot and darkening the nostrils to make them look distended.

The figure on the grey horse on page 68 is

Right: This black horse is mounted by a Trooper of the Grenadiers of the French Imperial Guard

The charge of the Scots Greys at Waterloo—
Sergeant Ewart seizes the colours of the
45th French Infantry. The painting of the
horses has been done with great skill

Painting Techniques

Napoleon. The horse is the famous Marengo, whose skeleton is at the National Army Museum in London. Napoleon himself is wearing his favourite uniform beneath his grey coat—the undress uniform of the *Chasseur à cheval* of the Guard. His marchals complained that he was the most plainly and scruffily dressed of his army.

Most military horses were purchased to conform to height and colouring within the unit. White marks on face and hoofs were kept to a minimum. Browns, bays and chestnuts were popular and

Below: Napoleon Bonaparte mounted on Marengo, one of the most famous of all grey horses

were often graded as to squadron. For example, the British King's Troop of six guns is graded from 'A' to 'F'—Troop 'A' have the lightest chestnuts, troop 'F' have black horses for funerals.

Some units rode horses of a particular colour, for example the Royal Scots Greys always rode grey horses, as did trumpeters and officers who bought their own mounts. The North American Indians favoured brightly-coloured horses such as pintos, piebalds and white-spattered mounts, which gave a broken outline against a background thus helping to camouflage them and confuse their enemy. The Royal Canadian Mounted Police breed their famous pure black horses on special stud farms.

1   There are four main types of marking on the face of a horse, though there are many variations on each of them and no two horses will ever be exactly alike. The star is set between the eyes and has four points.

2   The blaze runs all the way down the centre of the face between the eyes to just above the mouth. It may touch the nostrils but does not usually include them. A blaze is usually wider at the top than the bottom.

3   The bald face is probably less common than the blaze and the star. It covers the whole of the front of the face, stretching between the eyes, over and around the nostrils and reaching along the mouth.

4   The snip is the smallest of the facial markings. It appears just above the mouth and between the nostrils. More than one facial marking can often be found on one horse.

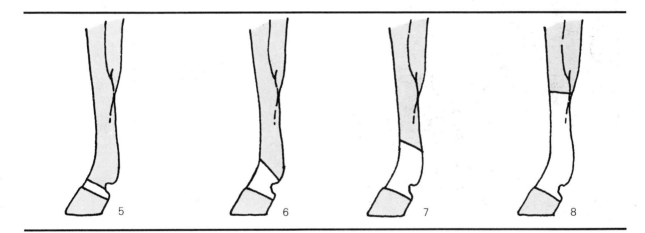

5   There are also many variations on the regular markings on the feet. The coronet is the slightest of the markings. It is barely more than a thin ring of white just above the hoof. Even that adds a touch of interest to a horse.

6   The pastern is the next length of white marking. The name of that part of the horse's leg which the marking covers is itself called the pastern.

7   Next comes the fetlock, which is the name of the part of the horse's leg which juts out. The marking covers this bone and stretches up to just above it. This is quite a common marking and may appear on more than one leg.

8   The sock, as you might expect, stretches up to just below the knee. The stocking stretches above the knee and is the longest of the common leg markings.

Painting Techniques

Project 3: Painting Artillery

Camouflage is the essence of painting tanks and guns, particularly in wartime situations. A variety of camouflage patterns would be used according to the field of operation in which the gun was active. For the desert, a pale yellow; for the Western Front, grey would be used.

The aim of camouflage is to hide the gun. Obviously this cannot always be achieved by actually concealing it behind or beneath something else. So camouflage sets out to make the gun as indistinguishable from its background as possible, by breaking up the outline. The rigid shape must be made to merge with the fields and

The German anti-tank gun camouflaged here had a maximum crew of between three and five, but it could be operated by only two men or even one. The two trails at the back were spread for support when firing but pivoted together and hooked behind a lorry or even a Volkswagen for transport. The gun could also be split up into its component parts and transported with comparative ease.

The British equivalent was the two-pounder anti-tank gun, which was later followed by the six-pounder. Most of the British guns were inadequate against German armour however, while this German gun was effective against most Allied armour.

trees in which the gun is operating, or with the plain colour of the desert sand dunes.

This can be done solely with paint. Break up the straight lines of the barrel and the obvious circles of the wheels with wavy patterns that cut across these recognizable shapes. Try to imagine that you are creating natural shadows.

Incidentally, when you have emptied out the tea from the teabag which you use for the basis of the camouflage, do not throw the tea away. You can use it for groundwork for a diorama. If the bag gets a little torn as you soak and drape it over the gun it does not matter: the netting used on active service would often have been well used and torn.

Above: A 30-mm scale model of a PzKpfw IV which was the only German battle tank to remain in production throughout the war years. It had a 75-mm gun and is here in desert camouflage as used by Rommel in North Africa

Right: This 50-mm PAK 38 anti-tank gun was used by German infantry throughout the war after its introduction late in 1940

70

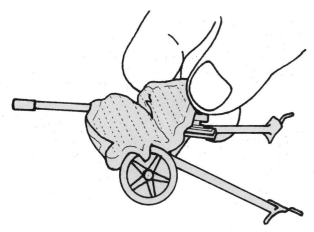

To camouflage the German anti-tank gun as shown in the colour photograph below, first cover it with an opened teabag. Cut open the teabag, empty out the tea and cut the bag open on three sides. Soak the bag in water to soften and then spread over the gun. You will need to split it a little to get it over the barrel. Partly mould it around the shape of the gun but remember that it is meant only to be breaking up the outline, not shrouding the gun.

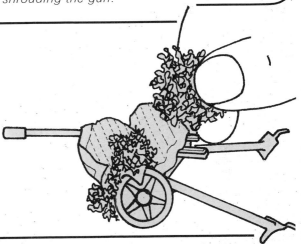

When you have painted the teabag with dull browns and greens, add brushwood in the form of pieces of lichen for extra camouflage. Place these over the gun to disguise the shape even more. If they seem too bright, dab paint over them as well. You can, of course, use only the teabag method or only the lichen as camouflage.

Simple Conversions

You can adapt any figure to your own requirements. There is no need to limit yourself to the shapes and positions you can buy. Exchange a rifle for a lance, make a change of clothing or even exchange heads to create your own unique figure

Very often you may wish to change a figure. You want a lancer instead of a gunner. You may want to change the uniform and regiment. It is a very easy job to make a simple conversion yourself.

Your best converting tool is the paintbrush. Many uniforms had similar cuts in different colours. Countries borrowed fashions from each other and merely changed the colour. Often a simple head-change and a repaint of the body can lift a figure across the guns from one side of a battle to the other. A French Hussar can join the British Army with a coat of paint and a British busby. A Coldstream Guard can become a private of the Essex Regiment with no physical modification at all, a brush is all you need.

Below: From right to left, Project 1 of the simple conversions shows a Dragoon Guard with his weaponry changed from a rifle to a lance; Project 2 is a conversion from a Coldstream Guard to a gunner of the Foot Artillery; and Project 3 is a Coldstream Guard converted to an Arab Guard

To do project 1,
do not assemble the carbine, which comes separately with the figure. Twist the right hand with the pliers so that the hand is at 90 degrees to the ground. Use gentle pressure only. The material is quite malleable and will not break if you are careful. The palm of the hand, which was previously on the same plane as the ground, should now be vertical to the ground.

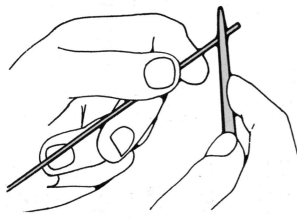

To make the lance, use a thin brass rod, about 2 mm thick. It is usually possible to buy a selection of various sizes of brass rod at an ironmongers or hardware store. File the point to a cruciform shape by filing flat on all four sides tapering to a point at the top

Make the bamboo joints of the lance with thin wire. There should be about ten joints. Touch solder the wire to the lance. Bend the wire round the lance. Run solder over the joint and snip off the length of wire. Repeat this at regular intervals and file each joint to shape.

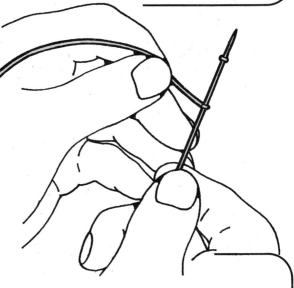

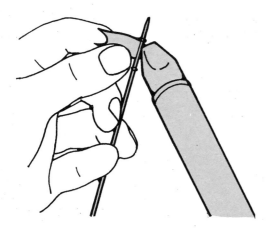

Use brass shim for the pennant. Cut to shape and solder to the top of the lance. Clean the join with a file. The loop for the lance, below the soldier's hand, is made from flattened wire wound around the lance and soldered, leaving a loop hanging down. Solder or glue the lance to the hand and base. Bend the fingers around the lance carefully. If you imagine the figure to be nearly six feet in height, then the lance should be nine feet long in proportion.

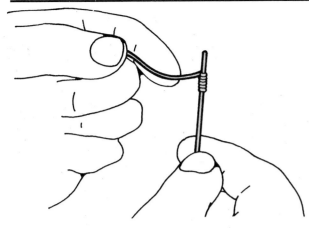

*To do project 2,
assemble the figure leaving aside the musket Use a piece of brass rod for the ramrod. Wrap wire around both ends, tack soldering it at the top and bottom. Wind up and down several times, making it thicker at the top end than it is to make the handle at the bottom. Run a coat of solder or adhesive over the wire and file to shape, but leave it a little rough so that it resembles material.*

Solder the ramrod into the hand and at the base of the figure. Although you do not need to change the angle of the hand on this figure, you will do well to wrap the fingers around the ramrod gently with your pliers, so that the Gunner looks as if he is holding it tightly. Remember to apply undercoat before painting.

Project 1: Rifle to lance

The unpainted figure on the right of the colour picture on the previous pages is a Trooper of the British Dragoon Guards in marching order, dating from about 1900. As you can see, he is carrying a carbine, which was common procedure. But at this time, as an experiment, the front rank of all regiments of British cavalry, except the hussars, carried a lance instead. A figure of this type with a lance looks very attractive and it is a simple matter to change the original rifle for a lance, as we have done in the painted figure on the extreme right of the colour picture.

The original figure is supplied with the carbine. The only changes required are the simple construction of a lance and a slight change in the angle of the hand. The colours of the uniform remain the same as in the original. It is always better to do any converting while the model is still unpainted, since if you attempt to convert a painted figure you will almost certainly damage the paintwork, especially if you use a soldering iron. The heat from the iron spreads very quickly through the entire figure. This kind of simple conversion can be done quite quickly with little effort and it puts a new aspect on an old figure. Just in terms of weapon changes, you can look at all your models with a fresh eye. Rifles, lances, daggers, swords, pistols, shields—you may already have plenty of spares in your bits box.

Project 2: Musket to ramrod

The centre pair of figures in the colour photograph on the previous pages shows a conversion from a private of the Coldstream Guards, on the left of centre, to a gunner of the Foot Artillery, on the right of centre. Both figures belong to the period of the Battle of Waterloo during the Napoleonic Wars. The year is 1815.

The figure is supplied with musket and pack. The pack is retained and glued on to the back of the figure just as it would have been with the original figure. The musket is left aside and a ramrod is made instead. This ramrod was used by the Foot Artillery for their nine-pounder cannon in the Battle of Waterloo.

As you can see in the photograph, there are also certain changes in the colour of the two soldier's uniforms. The Coldstream Guard has a scarlet coat with blue facings and white lace. The Gunner has a blue coat with red facings and yellow lace. This is an excellent example of the use of the paintbrush as a prime converting tool in conjunction with a very simple physical alteration. The resulting figure is markedly different.

In effect, out of a single figure you have created two regiments and so doubled your forces with a few touches of solder and some strokes of the brush. You can now make your own crew for a cannon in a scene from Waterloo.

*To do project 3,
reduce the bulk of the bearskin of the
Coldstream Guard by sawing with a model
saw about 6 mm above the eyes. Trim the
edges of the cut with a knife and file if
necessary. You may find the metal quite
tough to saw through but do not be
deterred. Try not to wrench the figure as
you cut but saw evenly.*

*Make the basic shape of the head-dress with
wire. Solder one end of the wire on to the
side of the head and then loop the wire
round to form a frame. Look at the colour
picture and you will see that the head-dress
continues under the left shoulder strap, so
make a wire frame for that end too. Fill in
the gaps with solder as described on page
51. If you prefer, you can use glue or plastic
padding.*

*This shows the inside of the frame being
filled in with solder. Make sure that you keep
your fingers away from the end of the
soldering iron. Cuffs, cuff-flaps and buttons
have to be filed off and re-engraved in the
appropriate patterns of two groups of four,
with three buttons on the cuff. Use thin wire
for the aiguilette. Braid and twist the wire,
attach it to the right arm and loop to the
fourth button on the front of the coat. Make
a good length under the arm.*

Project 3: Coldstream Guard to Arab Guard

This conversion is a little more difficult than the first two but still not too hard to make a start on, even if you are a beginner. The only part of the figure that really needs changing is the head but here the change is quite dramatic. We are going to convert a Coldstream Guard, who you can see unpainted on the extreme left of the colour picture on page 72 into an Arab Guardsman from the bodyguard of the Sheikh of Kuwait, who you can see painted next to the Coldstream Guard in the same picture. Both figures are from the 1970s.

The colours of the uniform remain exactly the same, despite the change. The Arab uniform was modelled from the British Guards of the period. But the change from bearskin to Arab head-dress is a distinguishing feature that seems to transform the figure totally.

In this conversion you will be using your soldering iron to build up a structure for the first time in this book. Make sure that you dip the iron in flux before picking up solder with the iron. Only by doing that will the solder run easily off the iron when you apply it to the part of the figure that you are trying to build up—in this case, the head-dress of the Arab Guardsman.

Make sure that you build up the solder bit by bit and not in too much of a hurry. Start in the centre of the head-dress.

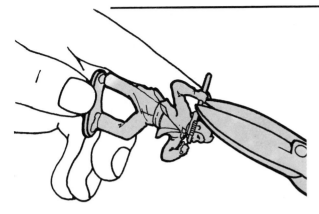

To do project 4,
assemble the kit with the lance provided and then work on the lance while it is fixed to the figure. Remove the excess parts of the lance with a pair of snips—that is everything in front of the left hand and everything between the hands. Leave only a short length protruding from behind the back of the right hand. Shape the length with a thin file to the shape of a dagger. This is a throwing knife so the guard is not thick. Cut the metal away to shape the blade.

Project 4: Mexican lancer (1864)

This Mexican fought at Camerone against the French Foreign Legion then on loan to the Emperor Maximilian. In a dramatic incident in the campaign, a company of the French Foreign Legion under Captain D'Anjou was cut off by the entire Mexican army. The company held out for a whole day in the ruined farmhouse of Camerone until there were only eight wounded survivors.

By that time they had completely run out of ammunition. In a desperate attempt, they charged the Mexicans—eight men against an army. Three were killed; five were taken prisoner. The body of Captain D'Anjou was never found.

Above: Nothing has been added to the original figure of the lancer. The necessary change is very simply made in this 54-mm figure

Following pages: The Highlanders breaking the line of Barrell's regiment at the Battle of Culloden, 1746

77

To do project 5,
remove the head of the figure of the
Scots Guards officer with a pair of snips or a
hacksaw. The cut should be made in the
centre of the neck, or just towards the
bottom of the neck band, as shown here.
Firm pressure should be enough to achieve
the cut.

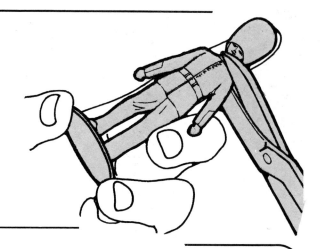

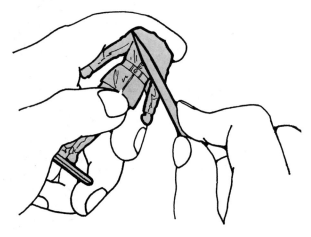

Remove all the detail on the uniform with a
file. Then remove the head of the French.
Infantry officer with snips. Try a dry fit
between the French head and the Guards
body before attempting to join them
properly. Trim them until they fit snugly. Do
not make the neck too long. You can always
build up the collar of the Scots Guard with
solder if necessary. When ready, hold the
head against the neck and solder together.

Shape the collar with a file and cut down the
top of the French hat with a model saw as
shown in Project 3. With knife, file and iron,
shape the hat to the distinctive forward-
tilted kepi. You may need to add an extra
touch of solder at the front of the kepi to
form the peak, if you have used a head from
your bits box rather than that of the French
officer.

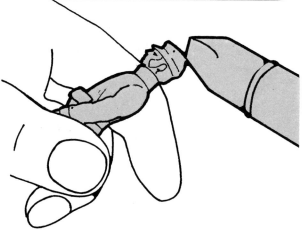

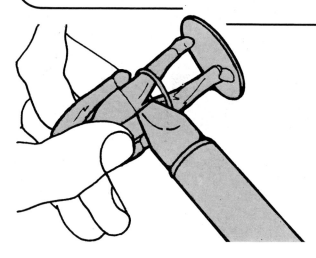

Lengthen the coat by soldering a wire frame
around the figure to knee length. Fill in this
frame with solder and file to shape. Use a
wire strip down the front to make the frame
for the front edge of the coat and fill. File in
the folds in the cloth. Add the sash by
making another wire frame and fill. Add belt,
pistol holder and ammunition pouch.
Impress buttons with a hollow-nosed punch.
Paint with grey, red, flesh, black, gold and
silver.

Project 5: Confederate Artillery Officer (1864)

Two figures are required for this conversion. To produce the Confederate Artillery Officer we have used the body of an officer of the Scots Guards in the 1970s and the head of an officer of the French Line Infantry, 1815. If you do not want to sacrifice a French figure merely for the use of his head, you may well have a similar head that would be equally appropriate in your bits box. So take a good look before you make any cuts into a complete figure.

Before you make any conversion, it is always worth having a thorough look through your bits box to see what is available. If you are at a loss for an immediate idea for a conversion but feel the urge to start work, then you may get inspiration from the bits and pieces that you have gathered already. Even when a figure is damaged, never throw anything away; it might always come in useful later.

The Confederate Officer was on the losing side in the American Civil War but that may well give him more appeal to many collectors. He is wearing the regulation uniform issued at the beginning of the war. Towards the end, when supplies were short, the Confederate army often wore captured Union clothes or even their own civilian clothes. Regulations about uniform were hard to enforce; you will note this from the variations of coat length in the print on the right.

Above: Scots Guards Officer, the same figure beheaded, and with frame for coat, the French officer and the finished figure

Below: Original prints provide inspiration and reference for conversions like this one

Complex Conversions

Once you have learnt the basic steps in making a conversion, you can achieve almost anything: a Zulu warrior from a Light Dragoon Officer, or Custer's Last Stand created entirely from figures of a British Dragoon Guard

Project 1: Dragoon Officer to Zulu warrior

Do not be afraid of the word 'complex'. We have only called the two main conversions in this section 'complex conversions' because they involve more work in detail than the previous conversions.

By removing all evidence of the original uniform and by changing the angle of the limbs and head, you can create a completely new figure which will be unrecognizable from the one you started with, as you might agree if you look at the colour picture on the facing page of the British Light Dragoon Officer of 1800–1803 which Alan Caton has skilfully converted into a Zulu.

Above: Detail from a painting by C. E. Fripp of the battle of Isandhlwana in 1879, one of the major confrontations between Zulus and British forces

Left: On the left is the Light Dragoon Officer from which the Zulu on the right was made

To make the Zulu warrior remove the head and arms of the Light Dragoon Officer by cutting firmly with a pair of snips. The removal of the head is the same as in Project 5 of the Simple Conversions. The arms should be removed as close to the body as possible.

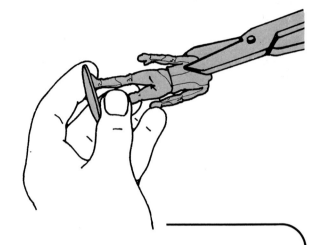

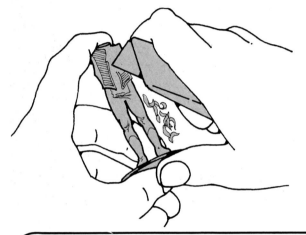

Remove all the detail of the Light Dragoon uniform with a knife and then a file to give the figure a really smooth appearance. You can see what the filed-down figure should look like in the colour picture on the opposite page.

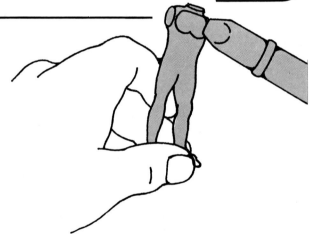

Build up the anatomical detail of the muscles with solder, as shown by the shaded areas in the diagram. Coat the areas of the pectoral muscles with flux fluid first and build up with solder a little bit at a time. You could also use either adhesive or plastic padding. File the muscles to shape.

Build up the shoulder blades in the same way with solder. File the basic shape to the arms and then reposition, fixing with solder in very much the same position as before. The arms were removed to allow plenty of room for filing the body to shape. File the arms to their final shape when they are on the body and remember the muscles. Change the angle of the hand just a little with a pair of pliers.

The most remarkable thing about this conversion is that Alan has transformed a clothed figure into a figure stripped down to bare skin and muscle. This is not as difficult as it sounds. The muscles have been built up with solder and it has been borne in mind that the figure is a very athletic, outdoor type, whose body would have been ostentatiously strong and lithe. The ornamental trappings have been made out of wire and solder and metal shim, in just the same way as any simple conversion would be made. Only for this figure you will need more time and patience and a steady hand with the soldering iron.

The rifle carried by this particular Zulu tells us that he almost certainly took part in the dramatic attack on the small garrison of British soldiers at Rorke's Drift in 1879. The rifle is one of the type captured by the Zulus from the British Army when the Zulus carried out an earlier massacre at Isandhlwana. The full story is both tragic and courageous.

In 1879 a British force invaded Zululand with a brief to subdue the Zulu uprising under the chief Cetshwayo, who was attempting to bring the Zulus under one rule and threatening the stability of that part of southern Africa. Led by General Lord Chelmsford, the British force consisted of 5,000 European soldiers and 8,200 Africans. Their plan was to form three columns which would fan out and come together again to attack Cetshwayo's royal kraal at Ulandi.

The centre column under Chelmsford himself advanced via Rorke's Drift and on toward Isandhlwana. The column was made up of 1,600 Europeans and 2,500 Africans. It camped on 22 January 1879, without making any special precautions for its safety. The camp was not entrenched and no wagon ring was formed around it. The common practice of camping within a wagon ring was known as camping in laager.

To make matters doubly dangerous, Chelmsford took out a large reconnoitring party, leaving Colonel Durnford in charge of the unprepared camp. In Chelmsford's absence, a force of 10,000 Zulus surprised the camp and slaughtered nearly every man. More than 800 Europeans were killed and stripped of their weapons. Chelmsford returned too late, only to find the corpses strewing the battlefield.

Meanwhile two impis, or regiments, of the Zulu army hastened to Rorke's Drift, which had been left with a garrison of 80 men of the 24th Regiment. There were also about 30 or 40 men in the hospital. They had little time to prepare any kind of defences before the Zulus started their first attack in the late afternoon.

The Zulus attacked from all sides, stretching the thin line of defenders to their limit. It was a particularly unpleasant surprise for the British soldiers when the Zulus began to use the rifles which they had recently captured from the 24th's regimental colleagues now lying lifeless on the ground at Isandhlwana. With their overwhelming

Above: By stripping down the original figure with a knife and file, you are left with a manikin

numbers the Zulus broke through the meagre defences and gained a foothold within the entrenchment. They were driven back at bayonet point. They broke through six times in all and each time they were driven back by the defenders.

The Zulus finally withdrew at dawn. They killed only 17 of the British soldiers and wounded 10 more, leaving behind 350 of their own dead warriors. Chelmsford arrived later in the day to relieve the exhausted garrison.

The other two columns of Chelmsford's force fared a great deal better against the Zulus. By holding their ground, they enabled Chelmsford to regroup his army and win a magnificent victory over the Zulus at Ulundi, only days before he was relieved of his command. His victory redeemed his reputation just as the brave action at Rorke's Drift gave back to his force the pride they had lost after the massacre at Isandhlwana.

The markings on the head-dress of this Zulu are not merely casual decorations, as they may look. They are regimental markings for the purposes of identification. The leopard-skin turban and earflaps form the basis of the head-dress. There is a third flap of a similar size at the back of the head.

The black ball at the front of the head-dress was

Complex Conversions

married regiments would have had different markings to the unmarried regiments. There is an enormous field of esoteric research here, and if you care to go into it in real depth there are numerous books and museum exhibits.

The belt and loincloth were made of animal skin, and you can make the beaded design on the belt either with a hollow-nosed punch or by painting it on. The leg ornaments were made from the long hair of the Colobus monkey.

The shield was used for camouflage as much as anything else and would usually be made of skin. On this figure, the ties in the centre that would fix it to the support behind have been painted on. If you have plenty of time you can make the shield of skin and use real ties threaded through the shield to fix to the support. You can also, of course, use real bits of feather for the head-dress and material for the loincloth and belt, although you may find it a bit difficult to lay your hands on a Colobus monkey. In this book we are confining ourselves to describing the methods used for constructing the figures completely out of lead but many converters like to experiment with all kinds of materials for the accessories on their figures. When you become more experienced you may like to try your hand with oddments of material.

For painting the figure, you will need white, black, red leather, brown bess, hardened leather and silver. With the large area of flesh, it is important to shade and highlight it carefully to give it a feel of shape and texture.

When you have finished the figure, mount it on the base with glue or plastic padding and spread groundwork around the feet. Sisal string has been used here for the grass effect and small stones have been spread over the ground as well, on top of a thin spreading of glue. The groundwork has then been painted.

While you are making and painting the figure, look closely at the colour pictures as well as the diagrams on each page. The diagrams explain how to make each step of the conversion. The colour pictures show you the final effect that you are trying to achieve. It is good to have this in mind while you are working on the figure.

There is nothing really difficult in this conversion and no reason why you should not create quite as splendid a figure as Alan Caton has produced here. The important thing is that you do not try to hurry the work. Do a little bit at a time and if you are using adhesive instead of solder let the adhesive dry thoroughly before you go on to the next step. You will be ready to go on to the next complex conversion soon enough. The principles behind the converting are exactly the same as those you have already learnt and you will not have to use any tools that you have not already handled when making a simple conversion. All you need is a steady hand and a little confidence, as well as a fairly clear idea of what it is you are trying to create. Always bear the finished idea firmly in your mind and keep any reference pictures with you.

Below: The decorations on the Zulu's head are strict regimental marks for identification

made on a cane frame, coated with clay and studded with small feathers. We have explained in the diagrams how to make the head-dress. The effect of the small feathers on the ball can be achieved simply by tapping the soldering iron lightly all over the blob of solder with which you have made the ball itself. The tapping of the hot iron will draw out the solder in a stippled effect which gives the impression of soft, downy feathers.

The feathers on the front of the chest may often have been of a different kind. Or they may have been cow-tails, or the tails of some more exotic creature. Different impis would have worn different decorations and markings: for example the

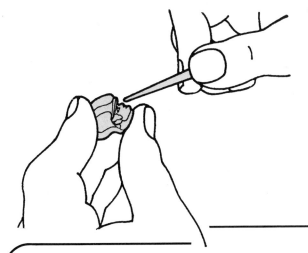

Some work must be done on the head before re-attaching it to the body. Add small solder blobs to make the cheeks fuller and file the nose more snub. Emphasize the crease between the lips by inserting a triangular file and make the lips slightly flatter by filing. When fixed, clean the head and add details of the head-dress. Make a wire frame for the three flaps and the turban and fill with solder.

For the head feathers you may be able to use pieces from your bits box or else cut them from copper shim, as shown here. Cut into the shim to make individual feathers and twist them up and down at different angles. Make a wire support for the chest feathers and cut the feathers from shim. Either cut into the individual feathers as before or paint their texture with thin black lines. Solder them to the body and the wire support.

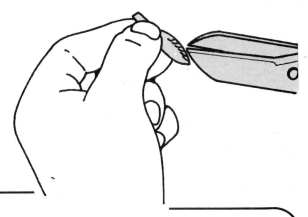

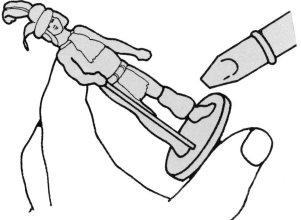

Make the belt and the loincloth from copper shim cut to shape, filed and soldered on. Bend the loincloth slightly to give the impression of movement. For the leg ornaments, wind wire round the leg below the knee and build up with solder. File to shape.

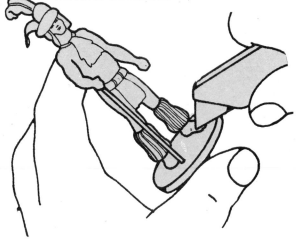

File the feet to their basic shape and then cut between the toes with a knife. Remember that the big toe is larger! Use a fine grade of wire wool for the final toe detail. A file would be too harsh.

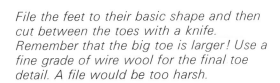

Use copper shim for the shield. Mark the shape on the shim and cut out. File the edges to make smooth. Make supports at the back of the shield from two pieces of lead strip soldered lengthways on to the shield, Leave a gap in between the strips in the centre of the shield.

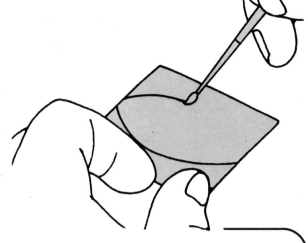

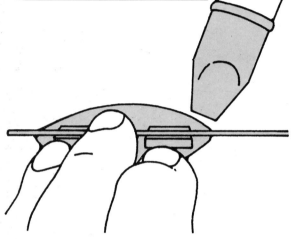

Cut the main support from brass rod and solder this over the two strips, so that the hand can grip right round the rod at the gap between the strips in the centre. Add decoration on the end of the rod with wire. The decoration represents the design of a civet tail wrapped round the end of the rod.

The rifle has been made up from the bits box, using two other weapons: the Martini carbine from the Simple Conversion Project 1 and a Lee-Metford as carried by a British private of 1890. The aim is to extend the barrel of the Martini carbine by attaching the barrel of the Lee-Metford to its butt. Cut both in half.

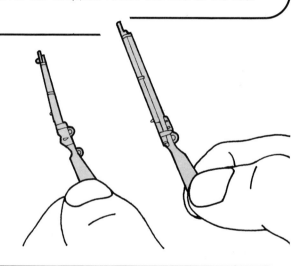

Solder the barrel of the Lee-Metford to the butt of the Martini, shape with a file to complete the join and solder it to the Zulu's right hand. Use brass wire to make the lances or assegais. Shape the points from a piece of shim and solder to the shaft. Then solder the assegais to the hand of the Zulu. Go over the whole figure with fine wire wool to finish off before mounting on the base and painting to look like the completed warrior shown on the right.

Complex Conversions

Following pages: The last desperate moments of Custer's Last Stand at the Battle of Little Big Horn, 1876

Below: The original figure for this group is the British Dragoon Guard already used in a simple conversion

Project 2: Custer's Last Stand

The five figures grouped around their regimental standard in the picture on the next page represent a dramatic incident in American history. They are making their last hopeless stand against the overwhelming numbers of the Sioux at the Battle of Little Big Horn, better known as Custer's Last Stand. The remainder of their company are already dead. The trooper who clutches the standard and the adjutant stretched on the ground are fatally wounded. The sergeant is out of ammunition. The trumpeter takes precious moments to reload. Custer himself is firing off the last few bullets in the chambers of both his pistols. There can only be a few minutes left before this last exhausted resistance is wiped out and the hapless venture passes into legend.

Starting with five identical cast figures of Dragoon guards, you can create the scene of the final five men to fall at Custer's Last Stand. The last moments of the Battle of Little Big Horn are recreated according to the popular myth, and using the most authentic recreations available in paintings and prints.

The background to the incident is a mixture of Custer's own character and the fraught period of the Indian wars. Custer himself fought in the American Civil War, on the side of the Union army, as an outstanding cavalry officer. He remained in the regular army after the war and was made a lieutenant-colonel in 1866. He gained experience against the Indians when he went to Kansas with General Hancock to fight against the Cheyenne, who were heavily defeated at the Washita river in 1868.

Another side of Custer's character expressed itself over the next five years when he lived a comparatively quiet life and wrote *My Life on the Plains.* This was published in 1874. Two years later, he joined an expedition against the Sioux led by Sitting Bull and Crazy Horse, in Dakota and Montana. General Terry commanded the operation, which was planned as a two-pronged attack, with Custer in charge of one column and Terry in charge of the other. Custer's column neared the large Indian encampment by the Little Big Horn river on the evening of 24 June, 1876, with Terry's column two days march behind.

Custer was supposed to wait for Terry and rendezvous for a combined attack on the Sioux. He decided to disobey orders and his impatience led to disaster. The following morning he divided up his column into three units and prepared to attack the Indians. Leading the central unit himself, with 267 officers and men, of which five were civilians and three were Indian scouts, Custer attacked the very centre of Sitting Bull's forces. Every single member of the unit was slaughtered. Among the only survivors was Keogh's horse 'Comanche'. For several years afterwards the horse was put on show at parades of the ill-fated 7th Cavalry, with a saddle on its

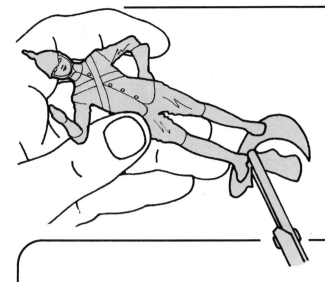

To prepare the original figure for all five conversions, first cut the figure off its base with snips. Cut off the excess material with a knife. Then cut off the head and both arms at the shoulder just as you did for the complex conversion of the Zulu warrior.

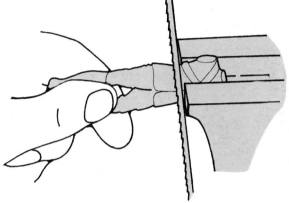

Fit the figure into a vice, without clamping too hard, and saw the figure in half at the waist. You will probably need to use a hacksaw. A model saw will not be strong enough for the thickness of metal at this point.

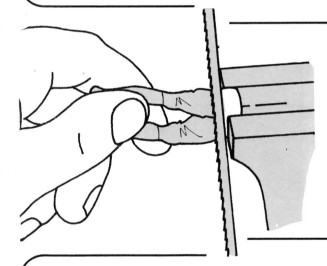

Using the vice again, cut the legs off at the hips, just above the line of the crotch. You will then be able to divide the legs quite easily with a pair of snips.

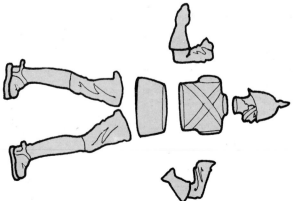

Here are all the parts of the original figure split up. It is advisable to prepare only one original figure for conversion at a time to avoid confusion. From this point on, you will be taking varying steps to create each of the figures, although some of the steps are common to them all.

Fixing the two halves of the torso at the appropriate angle is the first step with each of the figures. For Custer the top half should be inclined slightly forward. Apply solder to join the two halves at the front and then fill in the gap behind with solder.

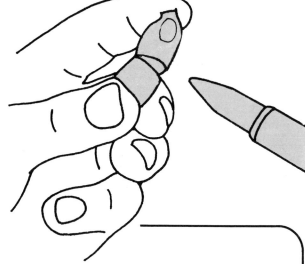

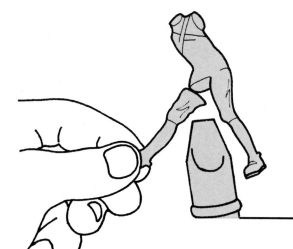

Fixing the legs is the next common procedure. For Custer, the left leg is angled slightly back, the right acutely forward. Solder them to the body and fill the gap. Bend the right knee by cutting a notch behind it and bending it gently with the hand. Fill the remaining gap and build up the knee-cap with solder. Then file. The left knee remains at the same angle. Try the figure for balance. It should be inclined forward a little with the chin approximately over the front leg.

File off extraneous detail from the remains of the original figure and then fill in the main creases of the shirt and legs with solder. The shirt creases are shown shaded on the diagram. Remember that the shirt is fairly loose and that the figure is twisted a little in action. Use half-round and fully-round files to complete the shape of the creases.

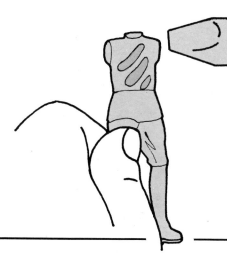

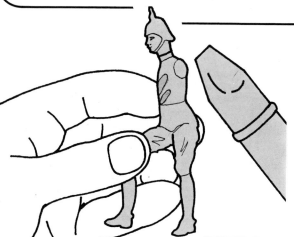

Trim the neck before attaching the head and make sure that the neck is not too long. Tack solder the head to the neck at an angle inclined forward slightly, so that the eyes will be staring along the pistol barrel in the final figure. Fill in the neck with solder.

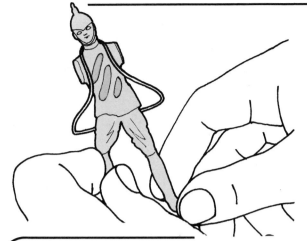

The tops of the trousers, the belt and the pistol holsters are all made with a frame of thin wire, which is then filled in with solder. First solder the wire in the appropriate shape to the body and then fill with solder. Use the same method to make the coat. Tack solder the wire frame to shape the edge of the coat and then fill bit by bit with solder. File to finish. Add a collar in the same way.

On the left arm the elbow angle remains the same as on the original figure. Only the shoulder angle changes. Look at the finished figure on the next page. Straighten the right arm by cutting a notch in the armpit and bending back. Fill with solder and solder the arm to the shoulder at right angles. For the frills of the jacket, build up solder and shape with files and knife. Solder wire around the top of the boots to create the new shape, then fill with solder.

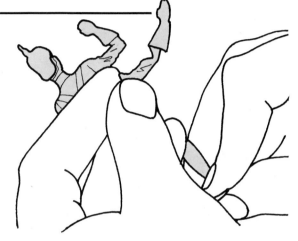

back but without a rider, in commemoration of the Battle of Little Big Horn.

There is an interesting historical footnote on Custer, which Alan Caton has caught in the figure in this group. Custer was famous for his goatee beard and long hair. The goatee beard is still apparent but his hair is unusually short. At his. wife's request, he had it cut just before the campaign that led to the battle. If this was a superstitious fear, it was well founded—or perhaps, like Samson, the loss of his hair also sapped his strength and wisdom.

The five figures have each been made from a British Dragoon Guard, the same figure that was used in the first simple conversion. Each figure has been remodelled individually and involves a separate conversion. You therefore have five conversions to make from one figure.

There are certain steps in the conversions that are similar throughout. They have been described in the first of the five conversions, which is Colonel Custer himself. These steps are shirt creases, trouser tops, belts, boot tops and heels, pistol holsters and pistols. None of these steps are difficult to do. They merely involve building up a shape with solder or a wire frame and using a file and a knife to complete the final shape.

Some steps are particular to one or two of the figures and these are described in the appropriate place. Colonel Custer and the trumpeter each have a stetson, although Custer's is a civilian one and

the trumpeter's is a military one. The sergeant has a neckerchief, the trooper has a flag and arrows in his back, the sergeant and the trumpeter each have a carbine.

After you have cut up the original figure, you must put the figures back together again in their separate poses. You should have no trouble if you look at the diagrams that go with each figure and also at the colour picture of the finished figure so that you can gauge the right angles for yourself. In each case the two halves of the torso are angled a little differently, except for Custer and the Sergeant, who are the same. The legs are placed back at different angles and the knees are bent in various directions to lend the figure action.

The arms are quite easy. In only two cases do the angles at the elbow change from the original figure. Custer's right arm and the adjutant's left arm are both straightened. As with the legs, fixing the arms at the shoulder is only a matter of getting the angle right. Once again look at the diagrams and at the colour pictures. The position of the limbs is obviously something which you can decide for yourself. You may want to make your group a little different from the one that Alan Caton has made here. There should be no problem. Just make sure that the figures look balanced and that the position is satisfying. There is no point in thinking too much about authenticity when you are portraying the last unrecorded moments of an action.

To complete Custer's head, you will have to remove the spike on the helmet with snips, cut down the long back flap and shape into hair, and carefully cut or file away the peak from the forehead. Shape the rim of the stetson with wire tack soldered at intervals and wound round the head in an increasing circle. Fill with solder and shape. Bend the rim. Build up crown with solder and file indentations. Add solder for beard, hair and to emphasize the moustache.

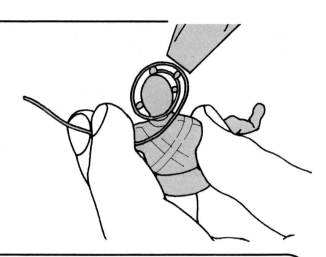

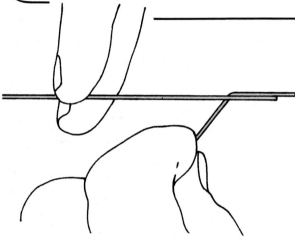

Build the pistols from scratch. Take a thin brass rod and bend down the end to form the rudimentary angle of the pistol and butt. Solder a thin piece of wire to the right side of the 'barrel' to form the ejector rod.

Build up the cylinder shape with solder. Form the basic shape with files before soldering the pistols to the hands. Wrap right-hand fingers round butt, then shape butt and add final touches such as the front sight, trigger, hammer and guard with solder and file to shape. The left hand was destroyed when removing the arm due to the position of the original figure. Build up a new hand with solder and solder the pistol into it in the same way as was done with right hand.

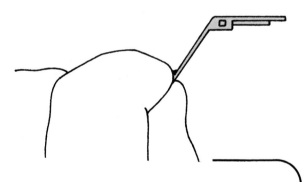

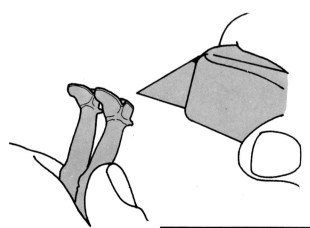

Trim the feet and cut in the insteps, although they will not show much on this figure. They are most needed on the prone Adjutant Cook and on the kneeling trumpeter. Solder the completed figure on to thin tin, so that there is a larger area for glueing the figure on to a baseboard to create a finished diorama of all five figures.

Above: The central figure of the group is Colonel George Armstrong Custer, a brilliant cavalry officer with an independent mind which finally led him to disaster. The events of the battle are shrouded in mystery. Some people believe that instead of being among the last to die, Custer was one of the first

Complex Conversions

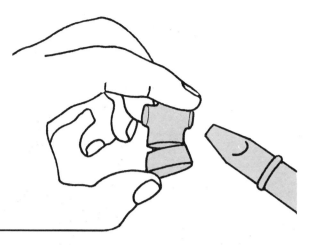

For Adjutant Cook, fix the two halves of the torso together as a first step. Work out the angle on a dry run before you attempt to solder. Look carefully at the finished figure in the picture. The torso should be inclined a little to the figure's left. Tack solder first and then fill with solder.

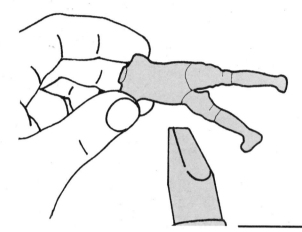

The legs are soldered back on at angles not very much different from the original. The right leg is slightly forward and to the right. Fill the gap at the hips with solder. Then bend the knees as with Custer. The right knee should be bent almost to a right angle, the left should be angled outwards. Trim the bottom of the feet and shape the heels as with Custer.

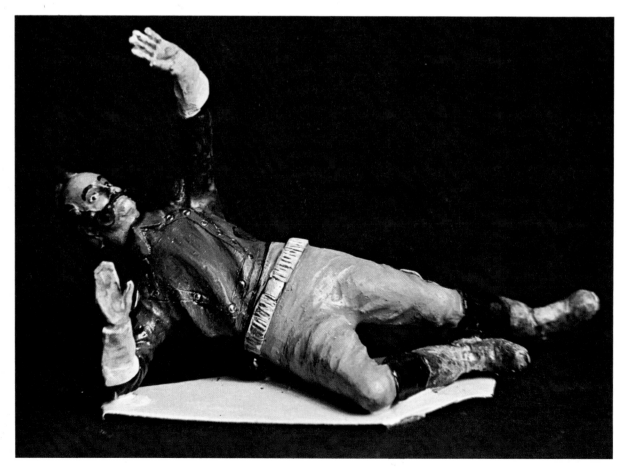

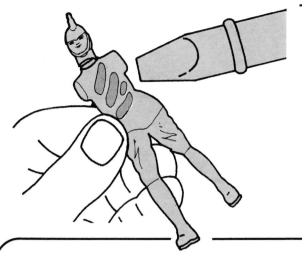

Position the head at an angle to the right. Cut away the chin strap and the top of the helmet. The adjutant has a high forehead so be careful when cutting away the peak. Use the back peak for hair shape, as with Custer. Build up moustache and sideburns with solder. Shape the hair with solder and tap it with the soldering iron to create rough hair.

Create shirt folds as with Custer. Also build up tops of trousers, boots, pistol holster and belt with wire frame and solder. Fix the arms. The right arm remains the same at the elbow and changes only slightly in its angle at the shoulder. The angle at the elbow of the left arm has to be straightened by cutting in to the armpit with a knife. The shoulder angle also changes. Fill gaps with solder. Make up the left hand with a wire frame.

This figure needs a lot of work on the left hand. Fill in the frame with solder and carefully shape the fingers with a knife. Make a wire frame for the shoulder boards as well and fill with solder. Don't forget the collar, and use a round-nosed punch for the buttons.

Left: Already seriously wounded and helpless on the ground, Adjutant Cook tries to ward off the blow that will kill him. There was a gory postscript to his death. Not satisfied with scalping merely the hair on his head, the Sioux also scalped his magnificent sideburns —an eccentric trophy of their victory

To make Sergeant Butler, solder the two halves of the torso together at the same angle as Custer's body, inclined forward. Solder the legs inclined forward and spread apart. Bend both knees a little so that the figure is crouching and braced. Fill gaps at neck and hips.

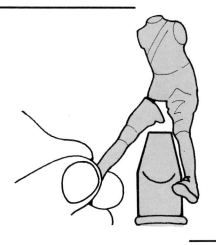

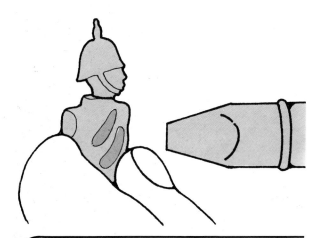

Angle the head slightly forward and to the figures left. He is pivoting to strike at an attacker with his carbine. Cut excess from helmet and emphasize the moustache. Give him more hair than the adjutant, so that it is flopping over his head. Build up the hair with solder and file to a natural shape. Make a wire frame for the neckerchief and fill and file as usual. Do the basic work as before on the shirt, boots, trouser top, belt and pistol holster.

Cut copper shim to shape for the carbine belt, and solder the ends. Bend it over Butler's head and solder to the left shoulder. Make a hook from wire and solder it to the end of the belt. Make buckles of wire in square section and solder them to the rear of the belt. File to shape. Both arms retain the same elbow angle as in the original figure. Solder the arms to the shoulders so that both are almost together in front of the body, leaving space for the left hand to be built up.

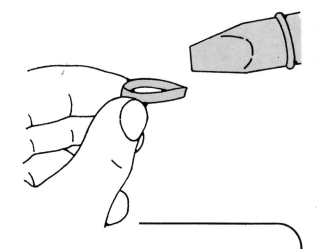

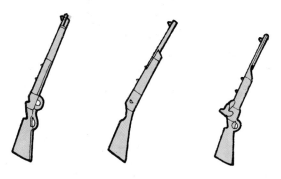

Use the original carbine as a basis on which to work. Cut it down to the bare outline and add the extra details of hammer and trigger guard with careful blobs of solder. Take great care if you are using the larger soldering iron for this work. It is better to use the smaller 25 watt iron. File to shape and solder to hands.

When you come to paint the figures, accuracy of detail is all important. You will need navy blue for the shirts, sky blue for the trousers, hardened leather and white for the gauntlets, and a lightish colour for the belts such as Humbrol's unbleached wool (MC30). The belts were hand-made from canvas.

There were strict rules for the yellow stripes down the sides of the trousers. Officers, NCOs and trumpeters had stripes. Troopers did not. The stripes down the trousers of the trumpeter consisted of a thin double yellow line; the NCO had a slightly thicker single yellow line, about 2 cm thick; an officer had a still thicker stripe of about 2·5 cm. Brass spurs should be gold-coloured and neckerchiefs should be spotted or plain red. They were purchased privately and were never yellow, as they have so often been misrepresented in cinema westerns.

For the blood on the adjutant and where the arrows enter the back of the trooper use crimson toned down and varnished to make it look fresh and sticky. Use yellow for Custer's hair and combinations of black and brown for the hair of the other figures. Custer's coat would have been made of buckskin. Use a colour such as unbleached wool with toning colours.

Use normal flesh colours on the faces. Give the appearance of unshaven faces by using a wash over the lower half of the face. Remember that the soldiers are exhausted and dirty with the heat of battle. Their uniforms may be tatty and torn. Moreover they travelled some distance before they arrived at the scene of the battle and have slept out in the open. The weather was hot and muggy that day.

To give an impression of dust and tiredness, paint the figures normally at first and then paint a dust mixture over their uniforms. Make this mixture from dirty turpentine, which you can mix in a separate bowl or save from a bowl you have already used for something else. Add a mixture of brown and grey paint to the turpentine and make a thin wash that you can splatter over the bottom of the soldiers' boots, the folds in their shirts, even on their hair. Be careful not to overdo this. Splatter a little at a time and then assess the effect before adding any more. It is always easier to put on more of the mixture than to take some of it off. Make sure that you make all the soldiers look equally worn and dirty.

The standard of the 7th Cavalry is now at the Little Big Horn Museum, which was erected to commemorate the occasion. At the time of the battle the standard of the 7th Cavalry was dark blue, as shown with the trooper in this group. Later, in 1886, the background colour was changed to yellow.

Painting the standard is a delicate job, for which you will need to use a very fine, cut down brush and an extremely steady hand. Do the painting before you bend the standard to give the impression that it is made of fabric.

Below: Out of ammunition, Sergeant Butler wields his rifle like a club and twists his body round to ward off the blow of an attacker. This figure has an excellent feeling of strength and movement

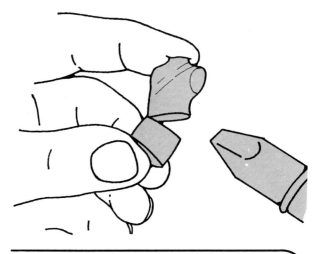

For the kneeling trumpeter start with the torso and solder the two halves so that the body is angled forward and slightly to the right. Fill in the gap at the back. It might sometimes help to imagine yourself in the position in which you want the figure, so that you can better gauge the angle.

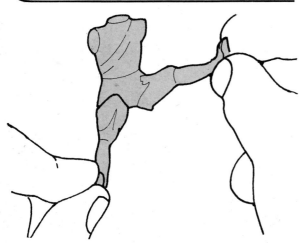

The legs are a little more awkward than usual. Solder on the right leg at an angle of 45 degrees to the body and the left leg at a slight angle upwards. Fill in the hips. Bend both knees. The weight is on the right leg. Remove this leg at the knee, reshape the knee and solder back. Bend the foot at the back with pliers. Now do the basic work on the shirt folds, trouser top, pistol belt and holster and the boots.

The head is upright and slightly to the left. Cut excess from helmet and shape the hair. Remake a new hat brim as for Custer's hat. Build up the crown and shape. Add to the moustache to make it droopy. Make a wire frame for the neckerchief and fill in. Make an open collar for the shirt with a wire frame outside the neckerchief. Fill shape with solder.

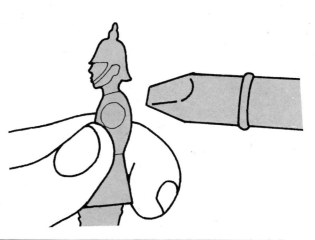

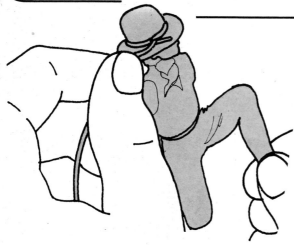

To make the hat band, loop wire around the hat and solder in place, leaving tie ends. Then refix the arms. The elbow angles remain unchanged. Solder the left arm to its shoulder so that the left elbow rests on the left knee. Solder the right arm so that the right hand comes in front of the body to grip the carbine. The carbine is made as for Sergeant Butler. Solder the finished carbine into the trumpeter's hands and shape his left hand to grip the carbine.

Below: The trumpeter of the doomed unit of the 7th Cavalry kneels to reload, pausing for his last respite before the inevitable end. He wears the regulation flat brimmed hat of the army whereas Custer wears the civilian version with the rim curled up. Essential details of this sort can be found through fairly simple research

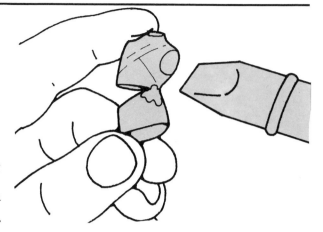

In the case of the trooper the two halves of the torso should be soldered together so that the body is leaning back and to the left. Fill in the belly with solder and file to basic shape.

There are thirteen stars arranged in a circle on the standard, and these mark the thirteen original states. There is also a United States eagle, the words '7th U.S. Cavalry' and the motto *E Pluribus Unum.* Good pictorial reference is always invaluable for any props you might need with historical significance.

Whatever little changes you make to the positions of the figures, make quite sure that you plan them as a single group, as Alan Caton has done. As we have said, there is no need to follow his positions slavishly. But the secret of a successful group or diorama is to plan it so that each figure looks as if it belongs to the group and relates to the other figures in the group. Of course, they will not all be looking at each other. But in this instance they do need to look as if they are backing each other up in the fight, and not just placed somewhere at random.

A variety of positions—lying down, bending, kneeling and standing—also enables all the figures to be seen more clearly when they are in a close group, as these are. After all your hard work you don't want to obscure one piece by another. Before you start any of your conversions plan very carefully how you are going to display the figures. It is best to make one or two sketches, however rough, before you begin. Try out several different approaches. Think yourself into the battle and make the figures look as if they really are fighting for their lives.

Although it is important in theory that the centre of gravity should be over the legs of a normal standing figure, in an action figure the centre of gravity will often be outside the perimeter of the legs. This may make the figure look off balance but it will be alright so long as there is some reason in the action of the figure that explains the off-balance posture. The figure may be reaching forward to strike or falling back in death.

Left: Still clutching the flag, the trooper falls as two arrows find their mark in his back. Perhaps the finest detail in the whole group is required when painting the standard, and a really careful piece of work will add that final authentic touch

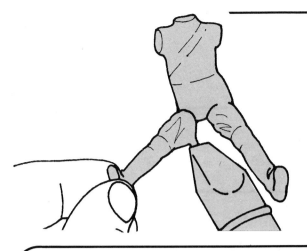

Both legs should be fixed so that they stick straight out from the body at roughly 90 degrees to the body. Bend both knees by cutting notches behind the knees. Make sure that the balance looks right, although the trooper is gripping the flag for support as well. Attend to the details of the boots, pistol butt, trouser top, holster and shirt.

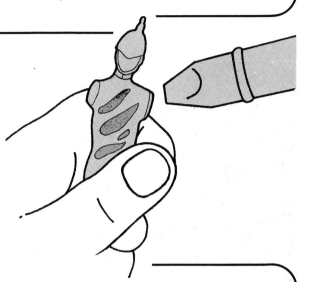

Bend the head to the left and back. Cut excess from hat and shape hair and moustache. To open the mouth insert pointed screwdriver into mouth and lever down slightly. To make the bandage, use a frame of two lengths of wire soldered on in parallel and fill in the space between them. Make a wire frame for the neck of the shirt and fill. For the arms, the elbow angle remains unchanged and the shoulder angle is only slightly altered. Solder to the body and fill.

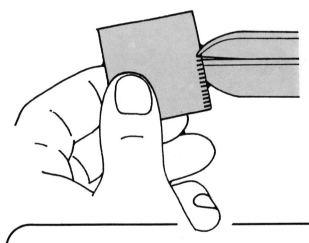

Attach the carbine belt as for Sergeant Butler. Cut the flag from copper shim and snip the edges for a fringe. Solder the flag to the pole, cut from brass rod. Solder the figure to its base, then fix the flag pole in the trooper's hands with solder, building up the left hand as you do so. Solder the bottom of the pole to the base.

Use little pieces of brass rod for the arrows. Make a triangular wire frame for the feathers, soldering the ends of the wire to the shaft. Use the smaller soldering iron. Fill in the feathers with solder and cut edges to make individual feathers. Use a pin-drill to drill holes in the trooper's back. Insert the arrows in these holes so that they are firmly fixed.

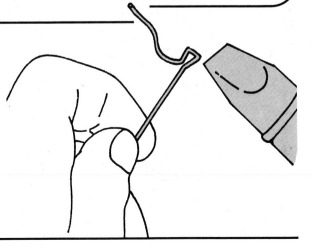

Dioramas

Alan Caton prepared the action-packed diorama below to show how effective simple methods of construction can be. You could buy these or similar figures in kit form or ready assembled and you need only the most basic materials to build the scenery

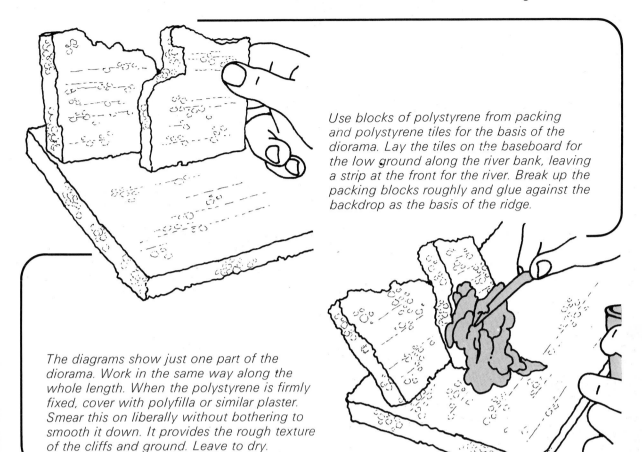

Use blocks of polystyrene from packing and polystyrene tiles for the basis of the diorama. Lay the tiles on the baseboard for the low ground along the river bank, leaving a strip at the front for the river. Break up the packing blocks roughly and glue against the backdrop as the basis of the ridge.

The diagrams show just one part of the diorama. Work in the same way along the whole length. When the polystyrene is firmly fixed, cover with polyfilla or similar plaster. Smear this on liberally without bothering to smooth it down. It provides the rough texture of the cliffs and ground. Leave to dry.

Project 1: French Resistance fighters caught in a German ambush

Alan Caton will always make slight adaptations of existing figures to create figures for his own dioramas. The two Resistance fighters in the foreground of this one derived from two figures of members of the British tank corps of World War II. All their equipment was cut away and the man in the water was hacked off half way down his thighs and then stuck on a small bit of tin to make him stand at the right angle. Both figures were dressed in sweaters and slacks, which was a very simple conversion.

The Germans are standard World War II figures, available in kit form. They too have been only slightly adapted. Some arm positions have been altered and some figures have been provided with different weapons, such as a Schmeisser submachine gun—the sort of spare you might well have in your bits box.

There are more German figures in this diorama than you may at first think. Look closely at the picture and look at the photograph of the whole diorama on page 112. There is one kneeling on the left of the ridge, one throwing a grenade, one being shot by the Resistance fighter on the bank

Left: Resistance fighters in the foreground are hemmed in against the river by German troops

and one firing at the Resistance fighter in the water. There is also one half-buried, head-first, in the cleft of the cliff-face just below the central tree. He has already been shot. Cleverly camouflaged on the right of the diorama as you look at it, there are two more figures firing from behind the bushes. And on the left of the diorama there are two Germans lying behind a fallen log, aiming a machine gun. It would appear that the Resistance fighters stand little chance of escaping.

Alan Caton's ingenuity is apparent in the German on the ridge, who has just been shot. As originally sold, he was a prone figure, whom Alan has set up on his feet in a most effective sprawling death fall.

As in any diorama, make sure as you plan the positions and physical movements of the figures that they work together as a group. In this case every figure is acting on or reacting against another figure. All the Germans are concentrating on the two Resistance fighters, whose positions in turn are responsive to the action. It is this interaction that gives the diorama its liveliness of purpose and holds it together as a single piece of action. You can even build up suspense—they might get away!

On the next few pages you will learn how to use other techniques to help you make your own dioramas—how to obtain different water effects, how to make trees and houses and how to use backdrops and lighting effects.

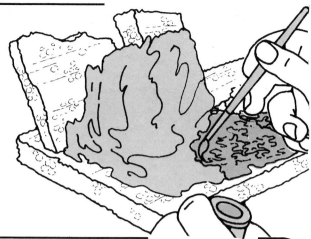

Paint over the polyfilla with greens, browns and charcoal. Paint the face of the clay cliff with khaki indentations to emphasize the cracks. Paint the bed of the river in the foreground with a variety of browns and shades of green, streaked and dotted with pieces of material to indicate pebbles. Apply glue to the river bed when the paint is dry and then place a piece of ripple glass over the river bed.

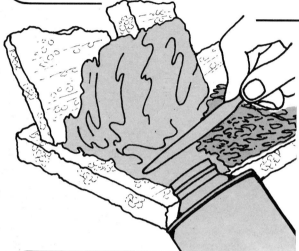

Animate and paint the figures. Try them out for position in a dry run, making sure that they are lined up against each other. When you are satisfied, start working from the top left hand corner of the ridge. Work a small section at a time. Work your first section up to the first soldier. Smear glue over the painted surface.

Before the glue dries, fix the soldier in position, spread your groundcover over the surface. Spread birdseed, sawdust, tobacco, tea leaves, whatever you are using, fairly thickly. Spread it also around the feet of the soldier. Work like this, first with glue, then figures, then groundwork, along the top of the cliff. Then work along the cliff face, using the groundwork on the ledges and in the cracks. Use a greater variety of materials along the river bank.

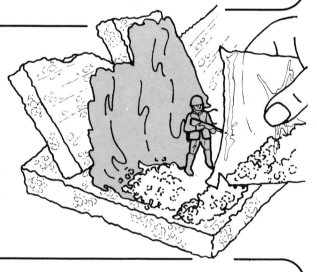

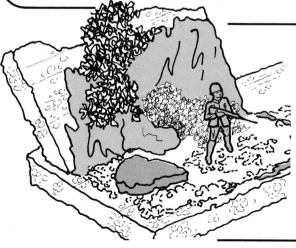

Go over the whole diorama again now to add lichen and trees. Remember that the machine gun group on the left of the diorama and the Germans on the right must be concealed from the Resistance fighters. Make the trees overhang the river for added naturalness. Bring the lichen down to the river bank. Use bits from a doormat or broom for the rushes. Use twigs for logs and sprigs of heather, thyme or rosemary for shrubs.

For many dioramas, the best kind of background is a large colour transparency which you can buy from many commercial photographers. Find a picture of a suitable scene—a sunset, buildings in the distance, a country scene. Fix the transparency in a curve, with the ends curving toward the front of the diorama. By doing this you will avoid the sharp angles in the back corners of the diorama that would be obvious if the picture is set straight across the back. Leave a space between the transparency and the back of the diorama casing so that you can place a light source behind the picture. If you cannot obtain a large transparency or find it too expensive you could cut out a suitable picture and illuminate it from in front.

Above: Here are the original kits for the German soldiers that Alan used in the diorama. We also show some of the materials used as groundcover: assorted lichen (yellow, red and blue), model railway ballast, pebbles, lucky heather, sawdust and plastic trees. Tobacco and tea leaves were also used. The substance of the cliffs and river bank were made of polystyrene and ripple glass was used to create the effect of a river

Dioramas: Making a Tree

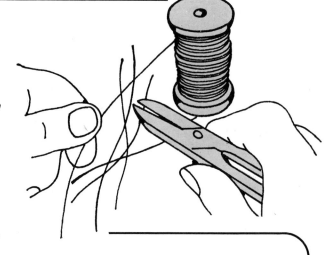

In Alan Caton's diorama he has been able to use plastic trees effectively, but it can be more fun and more versatile if you make your own trees. You will need a roll of wire, a pair of snips, lichen, tea leaves, glue and paint. Cut at least twelve lengths of wire. The thicker the tree, the more lengths of wire you will need. Experiment with about twelve at first and then try using many more when you are more experienced.

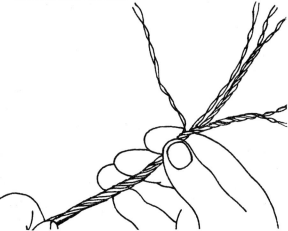

Hold the lengths of wire all together in one hand and twist them together in the centre. This is the main trunk of the tree. Leave strands at the bottom for roots and at the top for branches. Leave a centre core of wire at the bottom by which to bed the tree into the base. As you twist the wire together working up the tree, take out several strands as a main branch and then carry on twisting up the tree until you lead out another branch.

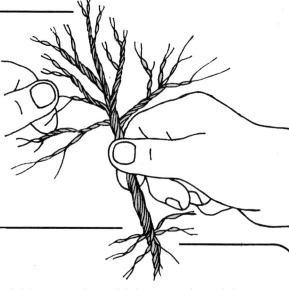

Create three or four main branches from ends of the wire twisted together and then take out smaller branches and twigs from single strands. The roots are similar but need not so long. Make sure that you create the branches in the round so that they come out from the tree at every angle and look as natural as possible.

Add two or three thick coats of varnish so that the grain of the wire shows through but is blurred to give the effect of bark. Undercoat and paint. This provides a winter tree, bare of foliage. For leaves, use pieces of sponge teased out to odd shapes and put in the joins of the branches. Then varnish the branches and twigs for a sticky surface and add tea leaves and sawdust. Add these on the ground as well, as debris from the previous winter.

You can buy many of the accessories you will need for making a diorama from a hobby-shop. For example the trees in the Resistance diorama are ready-made plastic kits, which are very effective. On the other hand, you will have much greater range of choice if you make your own trees from simple ingredients that are readily available in most homes. We show how to do this in the diagrams on the opposite page. Study the bark and branch structure of different kinds of trees—the spreading branches of the oak, the tall candle-like shape of the poplar, the denseness of an evergreen yew or the flaky white trunk of a silver birch. If you are creating a woodland scene, find out which trees grow together naturally.

Leaves can be created with tea-leaves and dried sawdust sprinkled over the twigs and then sprayed with paint.

You will almost certainly have to make your own river effects, but this is very straightforward. We show three basic effects in the diagrams below—still water, running water and waterfalls. Use some kind of household plaster, plaster of Paris, plasticene or polystyrene covered with plaster for the base, as for any diorama. Remember always to paint in some debris detail beneath the surface of the water. Water is practically never completely clear and the bottom is nearly always covered in rubble, rough stones, weeds, even tins that have been thrown away.

For still water in a stream, ditch or shell-hole, make basic groundwork higher than the baseboard. Add paint, pebbles and sand at the bottom of the hole and cover the hole with thin perspex or plasticard. Build groundwork over the edges of the perspex and overhang the edges with plants and lichen. The colours at the bottom of the hole must not be true because they would be distorted when seen through water.

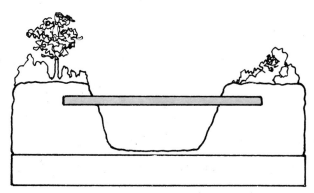

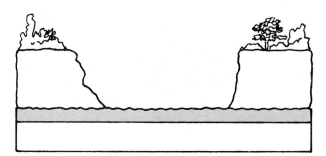

Use ripple glass for moving water in a river or fast-flowing stream. Paint the baseboard a dark colour such as very dark green, or even black. Glue ripple glass on the painted baseboard and overlap with scenic effects on banks. For fast-flowing effects, embed bits of stone in the glass and trail ground-up epsom salts around the rocks to indicate foam, or use teased-up plastic padding painted white as Alan Caton used around the figure in the water. Varnish stones to indicate that they are wet from spray.

For a waterfall or rapids, first build up the scenery to provide a sloping base for the water. Leave a channel for the water and paint this in the appropriate colours. Spread clear glue down the channel to indicate foaming water. Paint with white and add epsom salts. You can shape the glue down the fall with a small piece of wood.

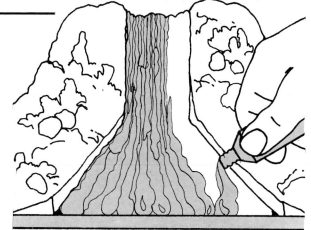

For the full, dramatic effect, the diorama of the Resistance fighters is best viewed not from above but from eye level or even from slightly below

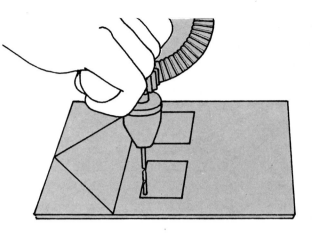

This diagram shows how to start on the narrow house and high-pitched roof in the colour photograph of a Napoleonic scene on page 117. If you are making the house out of ply or similar wood, first mark out the shape of the house-wall on your piece of wood and mark the shapes of the windows in pencil.

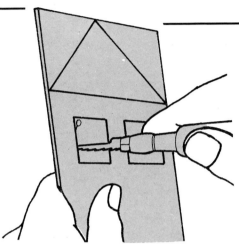

Insert a thin saw blade through the hole made by the drill and carefully saw round the window frame. If you have trouble turning the right angles at the corners, cut diagonally across the corner at first and then cut back into the corner once you have cut past it.

When you have cut round all four sides, file the edges of the window frame smooth. In many dioramas you can use clear plasticard or very thin perspex for the windows themselves. Paint on the edges of the panes of glass or trim down matchsticks for small fillets of wood to edge the panes.

Project 2: Napoleonic Scene

The French Napoleonic scene on the next pages makes use of a simple house structure made from plywood. Buildings for dioramas are not difficult to make. All that is required is a bit of straight-forward carpentry, using a saw, hammer, some nails, glue, wood and plaster. Perspex and cardboard will also come in handy.

To make the house, cut out all four sides from plywood according to the size you want. Cut the side pieces with a triangular shape at the top to provide the slope of the roof. Attach the four sides to each other with glue and small nails or panel pins. For extra strength glue and pin a fillet of wood down the inside of each corner. Cut the windows and doors before you pin the sides together. The diagrams on this page will show you how to make these cuts. If you want to have a figure looking out of an upstairs window, pin a fillet of wood on the inside below the window on which to fix the figure.

For staircases cut suitable lengths of wood for the sides and join these by short lengths for the steps. For a balcony, glue and pin a length of wood to the outside of the upper storey and add a balustrade. The roof can be covered with cardboard and painted. The diagrams on the facing page demonstrate how to make tiles out of cardboard. If you want to make a thatched roof, cover

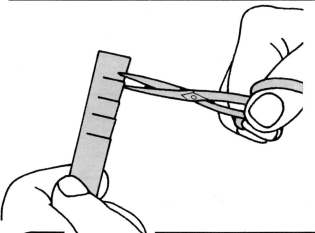

For tiles on the roof, you can either paint them on the roof-board or make individual tiles from long strips of paper. This is not too difficult and gives a very good effect. Cover the roof with cardboard first. Then cut into a strip of strong paper at regular intervals as we show. Don't make the intervals too regular. Old tiles were not always exactly the same size.

Cut out as many strips of paper as you need to cover the roof. Starting at the gutter, lay them layer by layer overlapping up the roof. Make sure that one tile overlaps the join between the two tiles below. Cut off the corner of several tiles to show that they are broken and leave one or two tiles out completely. When you paint the roof, add weathering stains over the tiles, around the chimney, if there is one, and beneath the gutter.

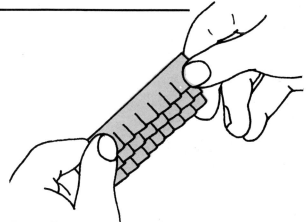

the roof with plasticene or plaster and then scribe on the pattern of thatch with a knife. Real straw would look out of scale.

Clear plasticard or perspex will make good glass for windows. You can also make curved windows from a straight piece of plasticard. Make a rough form to the curve you want from plaster or a piece of sanded wood. Then tack a piece of plasticard, larger than you really need, between two strips of wood. Hold the plasticard by the wooden 'handles' above the steam from a kettle until it becomes malleable. Press it down over the form, leave to cool and trim off the edges. The plasticard will retain the curved shape of the form. For the bulls-eye panes of glass that you often see in old windows, place some press-studs on the form before you lay the heated plasticard over it. The studs will then impress their shape into it.

Use toothpicks or sausage sticks for your own log stockade. For the round turret of a fort use a tin as the basic structure. Face it with plaster, plastic padding or filler. Build crenelations with plaster or little bits of wood or cut them out of the tin.

You may want to try your hand at a fort already dramatically shattered by cannon fire—an Italian castle or the Alamo. The easiest way to achieve the broken, ragged shape and texture of the walls is to build a basic structure out of wood, then cover this with plaster or filler both inside and out. Scribe this with a knife to get the texture of the stone or brick and build the plaster into the roughened shape of collapsed walls and shell-holes.

Many different textures for walls can be achieved quite easily. Sometimes you can give the wood an effect of plaster without using any plaster at all. The grain in the wood will often be sufficient if you merely paint over it. Or you can face the building with a variety of types of plasticard that are available from hobby shops. These sheets of ready made finish come in stone, large or small brick, regular or irregular brick, flint and so on. You only have to glue the plasticard to the wooden or cardboard surface of your building. Alternatively you can scribe onto the wood the type of finish that you want, creating your own design for rough stone or brick with a knife. When you paint the surface afterwards, run a thin wash into the scribe lines to make them stand out.

For many dioramas you will only need to make the buildings in half-section—to show a street background for example. For this you can use simple frames of thin ply or even cardboard. If you need lighting for the diorama, you will need to add a false floor beneath it for the battery, or add a box behind the diorama, as has been done for the French Napoleonic house on the next page.

Do not forget to add extra weathering effects on the roof such as moss and bird droppings; or graffiti on the walls; name plates, signs and street number on doors—as well as paving and groundwork outside the doors.

Dioramas: Lighting Effects

The basic circuit used to provide the lighting in the house on the opposite page is very simple to fit together and will provide most of your lighting needs. You can buy what you want from any electrician—a 1·5 volt battery, an on/off switch, a small light bulb and socket, and a length of wire. Wire them together as shown. You can fit several bulbs into the circuit if you want. Conceal the battery beneath or behind the house.

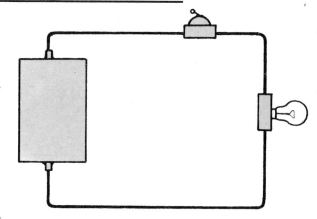

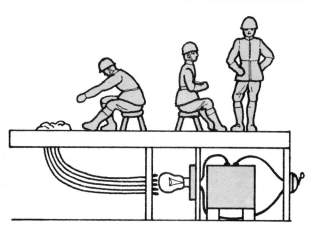

Fibre optics are clusters of extremely thin strips of glass that channel light. They are invaluable in dioramas for fires, lamps and candles. You can buy them from electricians in a variety of sizes. Set up your basic circuit and place the fibre optics in front of the bulb, clamping them in position. Bend as needed by immersing in hot water and bending gently between your fingers. Paint matt black over the fibre optic except for the tip for better concentration of light.

To light a diorama that is set within a frame on a shelf or in a bookcase, conceal the bulb behind the edge of the frame. Take care to get the right angle of light. Place the bulb low to throw flat light, with a pink or orange bulb for dawn or dusk. Place the bulb high for diagonal light, with plain or yellow bulb for hot summer sun. Or give greater depth by placing the bulb in the lower back corner behind scenery or a building. With simple circuits you can arrange to switch from one light to another.

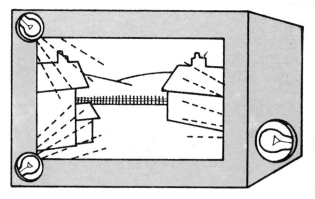

Lighting is not as difficult as it looks. You can achieve exciting effects by using fibre optics. For example you can make firelight flicker. Follow the instructions in the diagrams and then link another bulb into the circuit at a point just below the gap between the first bulb and the end of the fibre optics. Above this bulb and immediately between the first bulb and the end of the fibre optics fix a piece of card cut out in a propeller shape and mounted in the centre on a pin so that it will turn. The heat from the second bulb will make it revolve, which will intermittently block the light from the first bulb and provide the flickering effect that you want at the far end of the fibre optics.

Right: A lull in the campaign: this scene of the Napoleonic period shows a variety of French Infantry and bandsmen. Among the figures there are artillery bandsmen, light and line infantry. The house provides a natural setting for this diorama

Moulding and Casting

There is no aspect of model soldiers that you cannot do yourself. Your greatest achievement will be when you make your own figure, not just by converting an original but by shaping a lump of plasticene, plaster or clay and casting it in metal

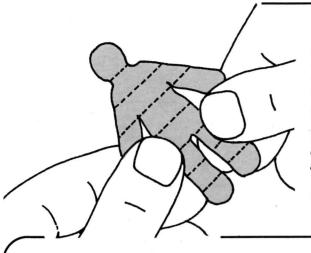

Plasticene is the easiest material for modelling, and Alan has used it here for a German standard bearer of 1935. First soften the plasticene in your fingers and then shape it roughly into the body, head and limbs. This should be easy. Get the proportions roughly right but don't worry yet about the details. This diagram also shows the approximate proportions of the human body. Taking the height of the head as a measure, the total height is about 8 heads.

Work on the head first. Use toothpick or sausage stick and stencil cutter or small blade. The basic tools you can buy for work in plasticene are ideal. A hollow-nosed punch is useful for buttons. Put as much detail into the figure at this stage as you can to save you working on the metal later. If anything, make the figure very slightly larger than it should be as the hot metal will tend to shrink very slightly.

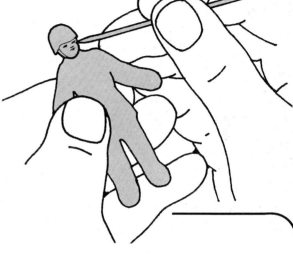

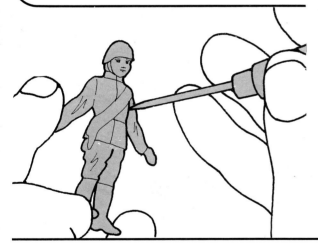

Carefully cut away the excess plasticene from the arms, body and legs, shaping the limbs first and then cutting in the details. Modern uniforms have less detail than those of the Napoleonic era or other important periods in military history, and are therefore probably best if you are just starting to mould figures. They may be easier to research from photographs.

Left: Unpainted Tradition *figures cast by industrial process show perfect detail*

Plasticene is not the only material for use in modelling. You can make a small clay figure in much the same way as the plasticene figure but if you make a larger figure you will need to build a wire framework or skeleton and fix this onto a stand or armature to keep the figure upright.

You will also need a wire framework if you make a plaster figure—pipe-cleaners serve the purpose well. For a fairly small figure, merely extend the wires below the feet through holes drilled in a plywood base. Fasten the wires beneath the wood so that the framework stands upright. Then build on a thin layer of modelling plaster or plaster of Paris, *not* household plaster.

Rubber solution can be bought in modelling

stores and comes in two parts to be mixed together. The saucepan you use should preferably be old and cast iron. Use a glass or enamel mixing bowl.

Using a plasticene figure, you can also make your entire mould out of plaster, instead of rubber. This can be dangerous. *You must make sure that the plaster is absolutely dry before you start pouring in the metal, or else the hot metal will blow back at you.*

There is a trick to be learnt when making the channel through which to pour the metal. You can cut the channel as described in the diagrams, trying to get the two halves of the channel as close as possible by eye since it is important that the channel is symmetrical. Or you can make them correspond more precisely. First cut the V-notch in one half of the mould. Dust powder on the corresponding area of the other half of the mould and bind the two halves together. Place between blocks and make your first pouring of metal. You need only pour a little. Leave for two or three minutes and unbind the mould. The hot metal passing through the half channel will have cleaned the powder from the other half of the mould in a perfectly corresponding V-shape. Cut this and then prepare your mould for a first casting.

As another alternative method of making the pouring channel, you can fix a wooden or cork plug to the top of the model before you start pouring in the rubber solution to make the mould.

Below: The main materials you will need for casting a model figure.

1 Rubber solution
2 Plaster
3 Plasticene
4 Old saucepan
5 Wood for box frame
6 Base for box frame
7 Solder: two forms in which you might buy it
8 Moulded figure
9 Bowl for mixing
10 Adhesive
11 Dowels
12 Rubber solution catalyst

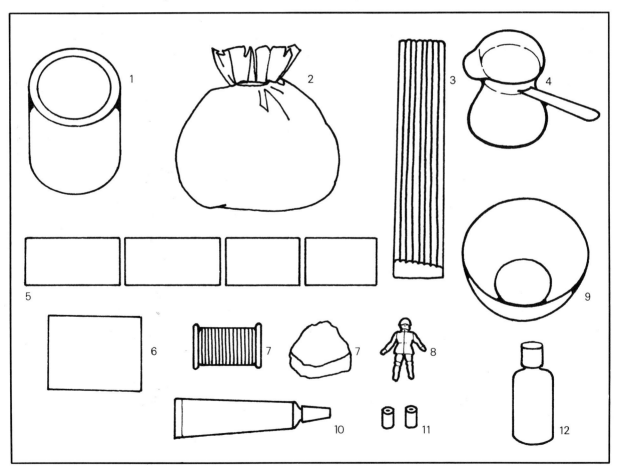

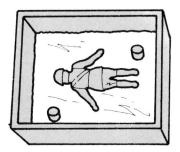

For the mould, glue or pin the four pieces of wood together to make a box with a pencilled line halfway down on the inside of the box. Place the box on the base. Mix the plaster and pour it into the box up to the pencilled line. Then place the model face down into the plaster and bury the front half of his body. Insert the two pieces of dowelling into opposite corners of the plaster and withdraw to leave two holes 1 cm deep.

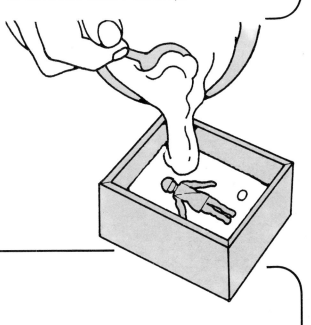

When the plaster has set dry, prepare the rubber mixture by mixing half the liquid in the bottle with half the contents of the tin. Mix in the bowl and follow the instructions on the tin with care. When the two are thoroughly mixed, pour the rubber solution over the plaster and the model. Leave to set for at least 24 hours or as long as the instructions indicate.

When the rubber is set, press the plaster and rubber out of the wooden frame or unpin the frame if necessary. Carefully separate the rubber from the plaster. You may need a knife to help prise them apart. Be careful not to cut the lugs of rubber that will have formed in the holes where you pressed the dowelling. Leave the figure embedded in the rubber. Clean off any excess clinging plaster.

Now put the rubber half-mould, with the figure still embedded, back into the wooden box frame. Dust the figure and the face of the mould with talcum powder very lightly, being careful not to block any detail on the figure. This will enable you to separate the two halves of the mould more easily. Prepare the second half of the rubber solution and pour over the figure. Pour at one corner of the mould, allowing the solution to flow over the figure from one side.

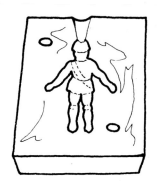

When the second half of the mould is set, unpeg the box and split the two halves of the mould. The plugs in the first half will now have corresponding holes in the second half so that you can fit the two halves together exactly. Remove the master figure. Cut a V-shaped channel in one half of the mould going down to the head of the figure. Cut a corresponding channel in the other half.

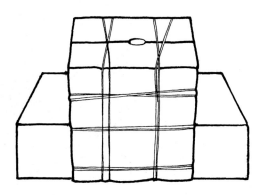

Warm the mould gently in a low oven for 15–20 minutes. Use elastic bands or string to tie the two halves of the mould together again, leaving the centre empty. Make sure that the ties are not too tight or they will distort the rubber and prevent the metal from reaching all parts of the hollow. Place the mould between two blocks of wood or bricks to keep it firm. It is advisable to cover the working surface with several layers of newspaper in case the metal leaks.

Melt the metal in the old saucepan. Nothing will happen for a while, then it will melt very quickly. You will need about 180 g (six ounces) for one 54-mm figure but always prepare more than you need—you will probably want to make several figures at a time, one after the other. Pour the molten metal carefully into the opening of the channel, filling it right up. Leave the metal to set for two or three minutes.

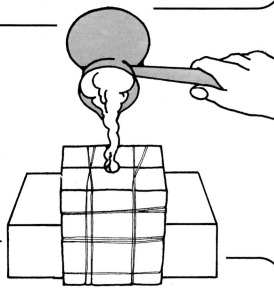

Open up the mould carefully as the metal will still be hot. Remove the new figure and lay to one side. Immediately tie the mould together again and prepare for the next casting if you are making several. It is important to keep the mould warm while you are casting. Finally clean off the excess metal from the figures and add the final detail with knife and file. In this way you can make many copies such as these Tradition figures of Lord Nelson, on the right.

Glossary

Aiguillette Plain or plaited cords looped over the shoulder and fastened to a button on the breast of the tunic.

Bandolier A wide belt worn across the body for carrying cartridges; also for cartridge pouches and powder flasks.

Baton A stick, usually ornamented, carried by marshals and field marshals.

Bearskin A head-dress originally made of the fur of a bear. It is much larger than a busby and is worn by grenadiers.

Bicorne A hat with two points, usually worn with the points to the front and back but sometimes to either side.

Burnous An Arab or Moorish cloak with a hood and sleeves.

Busby Fur head-dress worn by hussars, usually with a coloured bag falling over one side.

Cap lines Decorated cords used to attach the head-dress to the body, so that the head-dress could not be lost.

Cartouche A pouch fixed to the shoulder belt.

Chasseur à cheval A light infantryman named after a member of a select French regiment.

Chevrons Insignia showing the rank of a non-commissioned officer, or length of service.

Cockade An emblem, usually in the form of a rosette or bow in national colours.

Cuirass A breastplate, still worn as full dress by the British Lifeguards.

Cutaway Tailcoat with curved fronts.

Dolman A tight-fitting jacket as worn by the hussars.

Dragoon Mounted infantry soldier who is trained to ride but fights on foot.

Epaulette A shoulder strap, sometimes with ornate fringes.

Facings Details of a uniform, such as cuffs, collars and lapels, which are of a different colour to the main part of the uniform.

Fusilier A 'fusil' was a light seventeenth-century firearm. A fusilier was an infantryman who carried a fusil.

Gauntlet Gloves with large, stiff wrist pieces.

Gorget This was originally the armour worn around the neck of a knight. It remained in a decorative form as an emblem of rank.

Grenadier A seventeenth-century soldier armed with a grenade. At first grenadiers formed part of an infantry regiment but they were later formed into wholly grenadier regiments, even though they no longer carried grenades.

Hessian or Hussar boots Short boots of soft leather with a 'V' notch at front and back.

Hussar A light cavalryman. The hussars of many countries were modelled on the national cavalry of Hungary in the fifteenth century.

Impi A body of Zulu warriors.

Overalls Long trousers at first worn over breeches and boots with a strap under the boot. Overalls were later worn without breeches.

Pelisse Hungarian-style jacket worn over the left shoulder by hussars. It was edged with fur and often elaborately braided.

Pickelhaube German spiked helmet.

Pickers Ornamental decoration worn on the front of light cavalry pouchbelts. The original purpose is not really known. They may have been used for spiking enemy guns but their purpose was most likely for cleaning fouled touch holes of pistols and carbines.

Piping The decorative edge to collar, cuffs, pockets, around the jacket, etc.

Plastron The front of the uniform that is folded back to show the contrasting colours of the facings.

Sabretache A dispatch case, sometimes ornamental.

Shabraque A cavalry saddlecloth, often much decorated.

Shako A peaked cap or head-dress of very varied shape and size, originally Hungarian.

Sword frog A strap used to hang the sword from the sword belt.

Sword knot A strap used between sword hilt and wrist, worn to secure the sword when in use.

Tricorne Three-cornered hat which preceded the bicorne.

Turnbacks Coat tails folded back to show the colour of the lining.

Right: Napoleon's soldiers carry their wounded on their retreat from Moscow

Bibliography

Alberini, M., *Model Soldiers*, Orbis Publishing, London 1972.

Bard, R., *Making and Collecting Military Miniatures*, R. M. MacBride, New York 1957.

Barnes, R. M., *The Soldiers of London*, Seeley Service, London.
A History of the Regiments and Uniforms of the British Army, Seeley Service, London.
The Uniforms and History of the Scottish Regiments, Seeley Service, London.
Military Uniforms of Britain and the Empire, Seeley Service, London.

Beckett, I., *Famous Battles: Marlborough's Campaigns*, Discovering Books, Shire Publications, Princes Risborough, Bucks. 1973.

Blum, P., *Model Soldiers*, Arms and Armour Press, London 1974.

Carman, W. Y., *British Uniforms from Contemporary Prints*, Leonard Hill, London.
Indian Army Uniforms—Cavalry, Leonard Hill, London 1969.
Indian Army Uniforms—Infantry, Leonard Hill, London 1969.
Model Soldiers, Arms and Armour Press, London 1974.

Chandler, D., *The Art of Warfare on Land*, Paul Hamlyn, London 1974.

Davis, B., *German Army Uniforms and Insignia*, Arms and Armour Press, London 1971.

Falls, C., *Great Military Battles*, Spring Books, London 1969.

Featherstone, D., *War Games*, Stanley Paul, London 1962.

Foster, D. S. V., *Cuirassiers and Heavy Cavalry*, Almark, London 1974.

Funken, L. and F., *L'Uniforme et les Armes des Soldats de Tous les Temps*, Casterman, Paris 1967.
L'Uniformes et les Armes des Soldats du Premier Empire, Casterman, Paris 1968.

Garratt, J. G., *Model Soldiers*, Seeley Service, London.

Harris, H., *Model Soldiers*, Octopus Books, London 1974.

Harris, R. G., *Fifty Years of Yeomanry Uniforms*, F. Muller, London 1972.

Haythornthwaite, P., *Uniforms of the American Civil War*, Blandford Press, Poole, Dorset 1975.
Uniforms of the Retreat from Moscow, Blandford Press, Poole, Dorset 1976.

Kannik, P., *Military Uniforms of the World*, Blandford Press, Poole, Dorset 1968; Macmillan, New York 1968.

Lawson, C. C. P., *History of the Uniforms of the British Army*—5 vols, Kaye & Ward, London 1971.

Lord, F. A. and Wise, A., *Uniforms of the Civil War*, Yoseloff, London 1970.

Melagari, V., *Great Regiments*, Weidenfeld & Nicolson, London 1969.

Newman, P., *Militaria*, Discovering Books, Shire Publications, Princes Risborough, Bucks 1969.

North, R., *Regiments at Waterloo*, Almark Publishing, London 1971.

Paine, Lauran, *General Custer Story*, W. Foulsham, Slough, Berks 1960.

Richards, L. W., *Old British Model Soldiers 1893–1918*, Arms and Armour Press, London 1970.

Risley, C. A. and Imrie, W. F., *Model Soldier Guide*, Imrie-Risley, New York.

Taylor, A. *British Cavalry Regiments*, Discovering Books, Shire Publications, Princes Risborough, Bucks 1973.
British Military Uniforms, Discovering Books, Shire Publications, Princes Risborough, Bucks 1972.

Teague, D. C., *Modelling for Wargamers*, Discovering Books, Shire Publications, Princes Risborough, Bucks 1973.

Wells, H. G., *Little Wars*, Arms and Armour Press, London 1970.

Wilkinson, F., *Battle Dress*, Guinness Superlatives Ltd., Enfield, Middlesex 1970; Doubleday, New York 1971.
Antique Guns and Gun Collecting, Paul Hamlyn, London 1975.

Wilkinson-Latham, J., *Edged Weapons*, Discovering Books, Shire Publications, Princes Risborough, Bucks 1972.

Wilkinson-Latham, R. and C., *Cavalry Uniforms*, Blandford Press, Poole, Dorset 1971; Macmillan, New York 1971.
Infantry Uniforms, Blandford Press, Poole, Dorset 1971; Macmillan, New York 1971.

Wilkinson-Latham, R., *British Military Badges and Buttons*, Discovering Books, Shire Publications. Princes Risborough, Bucks 1973.
Famous Battles: The Peninsular War, Discovering Books, Shire Publications, Princes Risborough, Bucks 1973.

Windrow, M. and Embleton, G., *Military Dress of North America*, Ian Allan, Walton-on-Thames, Middlesex 1972; Scribners, New York 1972.
Military Dress of the Peninsular War 1808–1814, Ian Allan, Walton-on-Thames, Middlesex 1974; Hippocrene Books, New York 1974.

Suppliers

Listed below are manufacturers and distributors who can supply materials for military miniatures. Many local toy and hobby stores also carry these materials.

United States
Bivouac Military Miniatures, P.O. Box 12522, Kansas City, MO 64116

Boyd Models, 1835 Whittier Ave., Bldg. B1, Costa Mesa, CA 92627

C.S. & D., 731 South University Blvd., Denver, CO 80209

The Dave Casciano Company, 314 Edgley Ave., Glenside, PA 19038

Cavalier Miniatures, 105 Jamaica Ave., Brooklyn, NY 11027

Coulter-Bennett Ltd., 12158 Hamlin St., North Hollywood, CA 91606

Delaware Valley Hobby Distributors, Inc., 701 Ashland Ave., Folcroft, PA 19032

GHQ Micro Armour, 2634 Bryant Ave. South, Minneapolis, MN 55408

Grenadier Miniatures, 118 Lynbrooke Rd., Springfield, PA 19063

Heritage Models, Inc., 9840 Monroe Drive, Bldg. 106, Dallas, TX 75220

History in Metal, P.O. Box 451, Chargin Falls, OH 44022

Imrie/Risley Miniatures, Inc., RD3, Route 67, Ballston Spa, NY 12020

Little Generals, P.O. Box 8646, Kansas City, MO 64114

Tom Loback Artworks, 150 West 26th St., New York, NY 10001

Military Figurines Ltd., Box P, Pine Plains, NY 12567

Military Model Distributors, 3461 East Ten Mile Rd., Warren, MI 48091

Monarch, P.O. Box 4195, Long Island City, NY 11104

The Old Guard, Inc., 33 North Main St., New Hope, PA 18938

Polk's Model Craft Hobbies, Inc., 346 Bergen Ave., Jersey City, NJ 07304

Reeves International, 1107 Broadway, New York, NY 10010

Jack Scruby's Miniatures, P.O. Box 1658, Cambria, CA 93428

Sentai Distributors, 8735 Shirley Ave., Northridge, CA 91324

Series 77 Miniatures, P.O. Box 1141, Canoga Park, CA 91304

Strictly Wargaming, 3100 Bayside Drive, Palatine, IL 60067

US Airfix, AVA International, Inc., 6500 Depot Drive, P.O. Box 7611, Waco, TX 76710

Valiant Miniatures, P.O. Box 394, Skokie, IL 60076

WRW Imports, Inc., 3730 Wheeling St., Denver, CO 80239

Ronald Wall Figurines Ltd., 7370 Pasadena, St. Louis, MO 63121

Lou Zocchi & Associates, 7604 Newton Drive, Biloxi, MS 39532

Australia
Battlefield, P.O. Box 47, Wahroonga, N.S.W. 2076

Block, James, 5 Wurth Place, Canberra, A.C.T.

Mainly Military, 164 King Street, Sydney, N.S.W.

Canada
Derreck Miniatures, 96 Briscoe Street East, London, Ontario.

France
Guilbart, J., 10 Rue du Pont au Choux, Paris 3e.

Historex Aeros SA, 23 rue Petion, Paris.

Germany
Cortum, George, 2000 Hamburg 71, Koppenstrasse 6.

Kebbel, Harald, 8500 Nurnberg, Obere Schiedgasse 56.

Retter, Alfred, 7000 Stuttgart 75, Kleinhohenheimerstrasse 32.

Scholtz, Werner, 1000 Berlin 12, Knesebeckerstrasse 86/87.

Zorn, Dr H. G., 6277 Camberg/Taunus, Hopfen Strasse 7.

Great Britain
Dek Military Models, 71 Vaughan Way, Leicester.

Heroics and Ross Figures, 36 Kennington Road, London, SE1.

Hinchcliffe Models, 21 Station Street, Meltham, Huddersfield, Yorks.

Hinton-Hunt Figures, 27 Camden Passage, London N1.

Historex Agents, 3 Castle Street, Dover, Kent.

Tradition, 5a/5b Shepherd Street, London W1

Under Two Flags, 4 St Christopher's Place, London W1.

Willie Figures (E. Suren), 60 Lower Sloane Street, London SW1.

Italy
Antonini, F., via Lago di Lesina 15, Rome

'Geco', via San G.B. de la Salle, 20132 Milan.

Switzerland
Ruinart, P., rue des Terreaux 2, Lausanne, 1003.

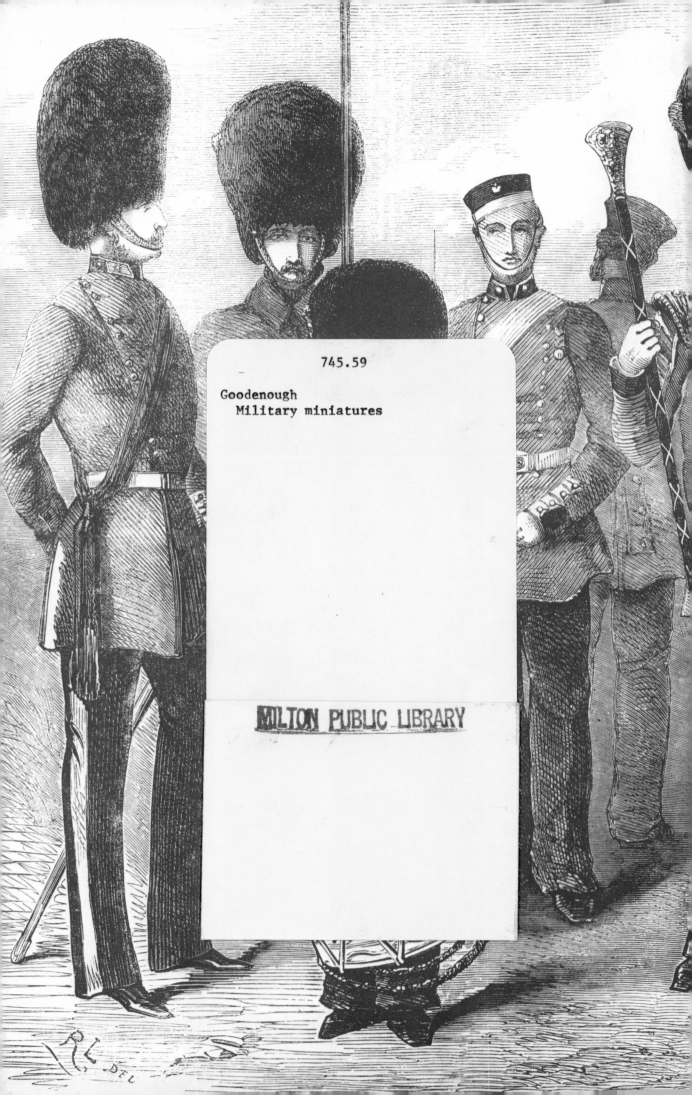